CHRISTMAS
with
Country Living

Volume III

CHRISTMAS
with
Country Living™
Volume III

Oxmoor House.

HEARST COMMUNICATIONS, INC.

Christmas with Country Living™ VOLUME III
©1999 Hearst Communications Inc., and Oxmoor House, Inc.
www.countryliving.com

Country Living™ is a trademark of Hearst Communications Inc.
Oxmoor House, Inc.
Book Division of Southern Progress Corporation
P.O. Box 2463, Birmingham, AL 35201

ISBN: 0-8487-1880-1
ISSN: 1094-2866
Manufactured in the United States of America
First Printing 1999

We're here for you!
We at Oxmoor House are dedicated to serving you with
reliable information that expands your imagination and enriches
your life. We welcome your comments and suggestions. Please
write us at:

       Oxmoor House, Inc.
       Editor, ***Christmas with Country Living***™
       2100 Lakeshore Drive
       Birmingham, AL 35209
To order additional publications, call 1-205-877-6560.

Country Living™
Editor-in-Chief: Nancy Mernit Soriano
Managing Editor: Mary R. Roby
Deputy Editor: Lawrence A. Bilotti
Senior Editor: Marjorie E. Gage
Senior Editor/Decorating & Design: Robin Long Mayer
Senior Editor/Special Projects: Marylou Krajci
Editor/Home Building & Architecture: Pamela Abrahams
Editor/Food: Cynthia N. LaGrone

Oxmoor House, Inc.
Editor-in-Chief: Nancy Fitzpatrick Wyatt
Senior Editor, Copy and Homes: Olivia Kindig Wells
Senior Foods Editor: Susan Payne Stabler
Art Director: James Boone

Christmas with Country Living™ VOLUME III
Editor: Shannon Sexton Jernigan
Associate Art Director: Cynthia R. Cooper
Senior Designer: Melissa Jones Clark
Editorial Assistant: Allison Long
Copy Editors: Donna Baldone, L. Amanda Owens
Illustrator: Kelly Davis
Senior Photographer: Jim Bathie
Director, Production and Distribution: Phillip Lee
Associate Production Manager: James McDaniel
Production Assistant: Faye Porter Bonner

Contributors
Guest Editors: Richard Kollath, Edward McCann
Editorial Contributor: Lola Vickers
Design Consultant: Susi Oberhelman

CONTENTS

FOREWORD

Throughout the year—and especially during the holidays—providing our readers with ideas for filling the home with simple, beautiful things is the hallmark of *Country Living*. You'll find that notion reflected in this collection of decorations and gifts. A house adorned with handmade touches reflects the celebratory spirit of those who call it home. So, welcome to *Christmas with Country Living*, where you'll discover an abundance of ways to create the warmest of holidays, both indoors and out.

Decorating with style need not be complicated. Our projects are as simple as they are attractive, and best of all, they require no special tools, skills, or experience. A project can be as easy as arranging flowers in a clear vase of cranberries (page 56), wrapping small boughs with twine to create smudge sticks (page 118), or folding a paper party hat (page 92). Many of these items also make thoughtful gifts. Our resources section shows you where to find all that you need to create holiday accents, such as the wreath of California manzanita shown opposite.

For tastes of the season, there are over a dozen cookie recipes, coupled with ideas for presentation. And you'll find a hearty Christmas dinner menu, with an emphasis on make-ahead options. After all, planning a feast shouldn't mean that you can't enjoy it, too!

We hope this volume of *Christmas with Country Living* enhances your celebration this holiday season.

THE EDITORS OF *COUNTRY LIVING*

TRIM

MINGS

$\mathcal{G}$ARLANDS

LIKE A STRAND OF PEARLS OR A SINGLE SWEET NOTE drawn out by a violinist, a festive holiday garland can be both exquisitely simple and elegantly striking. Combine texture, color, fragrance, and handmade charm for a natural garland that acts as subtle punctuation in any interior, drawing our attention toward a room's most pleasing features. Looped over a window or a mirror, a garland frames a view; hung across a fireplace, it transforms a mantel into a festive stage; draped around a doorway or cascading down a banister, it signals a welcome to the pleasures of the season.

The materials suitable for a garland are limited only by availability and ingenuity. Almost any evergreen can be made into a garland. Don't forget, however, that greenery is only one option in today's Christmas palette. Give tradition a gentle nudge with garlands made of anything from chili peppers to dried hydrangeas.

A living symbol of the traditions that connect each Christmas to the next, a graceful garland is also a beautiful reminder of the seasonal ties that bind.

The wide doorway and transom of a 150-year-old Mississippi plantation cottage (opposite) is outlined in ropes of fresh pine trimmings. An early 1800s grain-painted case clock wears a crown of holly and juniper. Overleaf: A pine garland in the parlor draws attention to the room's architectural symmetry.

PINE GARLAND

1   You will need scissors, natural jute or other substantial cord, green waxed florist's twine, garden pruners, and fresh pine boughs. Cut a length of jute to the desired length of your garland, allowing extra if you want the garland to puddle on the floor. (Vines and evergreen garlands in 25-foot lengths will be ample for most doors.)

2   Tie one end of the jute to a spool of twine. Lay pine boughs on the jute and then wrap them securely with twine. Add overlapping boughs and continue to wrap until the desired fullness is achieved. Knot the ends of the jute and the twine to secure.

3   Use florist's wire to hang the garland, attaching it to cup hooks or to small nails tacked into the door molding or into the wall.

Cones of the California sugar pine, used above to decorate a mantel, can grow to more than a foot in length. To create this striking natural garland, the cones were knotted along a piece of string and then anchored to the mantel with small nails; sprigs of cedar and an arrangement of oranges and lemons top the display. Opposite: A double strand of pinecones is finished off at each end with strings of firecracker red chili peppers.

T O   C R E A T E

PINECONE GARLAND

1 Gather or purchase pinecones. You will need about a dozen medium-sized pinecones per foot of garland (see Resources on page 156). Other materials include 22-gauge florist's wire, green waxed florist's twine, needlenose pliers, a drill fitted with a $\frac{7}{64}$" or $\frac{1}{8}$" bit, and scissors.

2 Make a jumbo threading needle by bending one end of the wire over one end of the twine and then crimping with the pliers to secure.

3 Drill a hole through the center of each pinecone as shown and thread each pinecone onto the twine until the desired length is achieved. Tie off the ends with double knots and clip the excess. To hang the garland, hammer small nails into the door or the wall, spacing evenly. Using florist's wire, attach the garland to the nails.

ARTICHOKE GARLAND

1 You will need two whole artichokes per foot and a half of garland (overleaf: for this garland, you will also need ten lady apples). To make the artichoke garland, gather a kitchen knife, a cutting board, a large-eyed darning needle, and natural florist's twine.

2 Cut artichokes in half lengthwise, as shown, and set aside. Artichokes will naturally dry with purplish highlights in a few days. (Artichokes and lady apples can last up to four weeks. To preserve the natural color longer, keep them away from heat.)

3 Thread the needle with twine and knot one end. For the artichoke garland, string the halves onto the twine and knot the twine at each side of each artichoke stem. Continue in this manner, spacing artichokes approximately 5" apart and alternating the direction of the artichoke halves. (For the artichoke and lady apple garland, alternate two lady apples and one artichoke half until the desired length is achieved.) To make a hanger at each end of the garland, knot the twine and fold it into a loop; then knot it again.

WINTER WREATHS

THE CHRISTMAS SEASON OFFICIALLY BEGINS when the holiday wreath goes up on the front door. But with something as appealing as a wreath, why stop with just one? It's quick and easy to create several out of almost any material. These charming circles can be as formal or as casual as settings require.

Wreaths that make use of local materials and regional traditions add unique personality to seasonal decorating. Circles of fiery dried chili peppers, for example, have a distinct Southwestern feel, and a combination of spruce and bare birch twigs brings home the snowy North. For a dash of color, include pepper berries, misty blue juniper and privet berries, or clusters of crab apples. Even a simple unadorned evergreen wreath can be crafted from a wide variety of easy-to-find materials. In addition to the more traditional boxwood and fir, use broadleafed varieties, such as laurel, eucalyptus, and variegated holly.

Whether hung on the front door, propped against a window, or incorporated into a centerpiece, a simple wreath makes a delightful first impression that lasts the whole season long.

A casual wreath of manzanita and seeded eucalyptus (above) punctuates winter's landscape. Opposite: A snowy garden cherub is warmed by a circle of bright pepper berries. In cool climates, outdoor wreaths will stay fresh throughout the season. In warm regions—or for indoor wreaths—mix in some dried materials.

A red bandanna replaces the traditional bow on a wreath of dried peppers (top, left); a simple round of strawberry corn (bottom, left) hangs against a weathered door. Both wreaths were built on a double-wire frame and secured with florist's wire. For the pepper wreath, use several dozen peppers tied at alternating angles; for the strawberry corn wreath, you will need approximately three dozen ears (for ordering information on strawberry corn, see Resources on page 156). Opposite: A miniature boxwood wreath makes a whimsical accent on a vintage birdcage, dressed for the season in white pine.

A loose wreath of pepper berries (above) brightens a beadboard wall. Lightweight pepper berries dry in place and last for months. For a virtually weightless wreath that is easy to hang, use hot glue to secure pepper-berry stems to a foam form. Opposite: Late afternoon sun dapples a Santa Fe wall with the shadows cast by a piñon wreath, hung on a weathered ladder.

SWAGS

EARLY EUROPEANS USED TO HANG EVERGREEN BOUGHS on their doors as an invitation for passing spirits to take shelter from winter winds. Centuries later, a swag of greenery is still a welcome sight. Almost limitless in design, a cascading swag is a unique and versatile alternative to a wreath or a garland.

The word swag is derived from an ancient Scandinavian word for "swing." At its simplest, a swag is no more than cuttings of fresh greenery or other natural materials bound together at the stem end. A classic swag hangs downward, often combining several types of greens in one loose arrangement. Flat, spreading branches—pine, balsam, magnolia, or similar local material—make the best base for a large-scale swag. Pinecones, clusters of berries, and dried fruits are easy to add with florist's wire. Tied with a twist of twine or ribbon, the swag is ready to hang indoors or outdoors.

But no matter how you hang it, a swag welcomes the spirit of the season.

The door of an 1820s house in Kennebunk, Maine, is dressed with a gathering of evergreens and pinecones. The understatement of the all-natural swag is well suited to the elegant simplicity of the New England facade. Swags such as this can be dressed up with ribbons and other embellishments for a more lavish effect.

An upright spray of variegated holly leaves with berries is complemented by a simple birch-bark pocket (top, right). Use floral vials if the container is not waterproof. A cone is wrapped in grapevine and filled with sprays of colorful seeded eucalyptus and galax (bottom, right). Miniature swags are easy to hang outside or inside and are especially charming when used in unexpected places. Opposite: A poignant reminder of summer, this snow-dusted arrangement of pine boughs and dried hydrangea blossoms decorates a weathered barn door in New York's Catskills region.

TO CREATE

BASIC SWAG

1 Collect the desired natural materials. We used sage, piñon, and juniper, but any evergreen or dried natural will work. Select the material for binding. We used raffia; ribbon and twine are good choices, too. You will also need garden pruners, florist's wire, and scissors.

2 Trim the naturals into varying lengths with the pruners. Using florist's wire, bind the stems together to form one unit. To make a wire hanging loop, pass a length of wire around the center of the bound stems and then bring the ends together at the back of the swag. Twist the wire ends together and loop them back on themselves, twisting again to form a sturdy loop.

3 Top the swag with a decorative band, allowing enough length to wrap around the stems (about ¾ yard). Handling several lengths of raffia as one, twist them into a single band. Wrap the band around the stems, concealing the wire but not the hanger. Tie the band in a knot.

4 Secure the band at both loose ends with a single piece of raffia. Hang the swag on a door or anywhere you would normally hang a wreath.

TURALS

$\mathcal{W}$INTER $\mathcal{B}$LOOMS

WHEN DAYS GROW SHORT and the winter landscape becomes stark and still, fragrant blossoms fill the house with the delicate promise of spring. Plants have always been a symbol of renewal, repeating the sense of wonder that is at the heart of the Christmas season. Fresh flowers have a place of honor in any holiday home—whether potted or cut, massed in a lavish arrangement or displayed singly in delicate containers.

There's a profound pleasure in working with natural materials. Handling them—as well as nurturing and arranging them—gives us a reason to slow down and to enjoy the season. Each plant provides its unique gift of color, texture, and fragrance, from the subtle earthy scent of fresh moss to the distinctive perfume of fresh roses. Flowering plants, such as poinsettia and kalanchoe, will last into the new year with minimum care. And when it comes to ease, bulbs are hard to beat. Amaryllis and narcissus, two holiday classics, provide a certain drama, changing visibly day by day.

Flowers, once a luxury enjoyed at Christmastime only by the wealthy, are a staple of special-occasion decorating.

A dainty cluster of fresh flowers in a julep cup (above) lends its beauty to each place setting. Opposite: On the mantel, a boxwood wreath and garland, pillar candles, and a lavish spray of white tulips combine to make an elegant variation on the traditional white Christmas.

POINSETTIAS

A native of Mexico, *Euphorbia pulcherrima*, or poinsettia, flourishes naturally in the forested ravines and hillsides of the Mexican highlands, where plants can grow up to 16 feet. Joel Robert Poinsett, an American diplomat to Mexico, brought back cuttings in the 1820s, but it was only in this century, when new colorful and compact varieties were developed, that the poinsettia became a Christmas classic.

The poinsettia's true flowers are actually the tight cluster of yellow buds at the center of petal-like bracts, which change color as the daylight hours shorten with the approach of winter. Although they are hearty, poinsettias thrive in temperatures between 60 and 70 degrees and in filtered or indirect sunlight.

The poinsettia has been a Christmas staple since the 1920s, when a California grower developed today's hardy varieties. Red poinsettias, like the ones above, are traditional favorites. Opposite: Tucked into a birch-bark basket, the gentle shadings of a pristine white poinsettia contrast with the variegated greens of cedar and moss.

Create your own lovely and surprising combinations of flowers and foliage, such as teaming white poinsettias with branches of white popcorn berries. Poinsettias look as beautiful presented as a single cut stem as they do en masse. For a variation on the traditional potted poinsettia, snip the blooms and display them in coordinating bud vases. To prolong the flowers' life, singe stem ends with a candle flame before placing them in water. Stretch your budget by mixing fresh blooms with dried materials or fruits. And remember that single-color displays have impact—a basket of all-white poinsettias is at once finished and striking, as are a few white roses in a piece of milk glass or a spray of white lilies in a tall glass vase.

RANUNCULI

A relative of the buttercup, the ranunculus is a common wildflower in parts of Europe. The Latin name *Ranunculaceae* means "little frog," perhaps a reference to the marshy lowlands in which the plant flourishes. Most of these flowers you see at florist's shops in America, however, are cultivated commercially in California, where the colorful fields of nodding blooms have become tourist attractions.

The tight, full blossoms and papery petals of the ranunculus look like a cross between a rose and a peony. Flowers come in white, shades of yellow and gold, orange, pink, and red. They are abundant at the florist in the winter, when their prices are at their best.

Because of their free-form nature, ranunculi often need gentle support. To keep the flowers in line without sacrificing spontaneity, pack the flowers' container tightly so that stems gain support from each other; or place a piece of chicken wire or a crisscross of floral tape over the mouth of the container before inserting the flowers. In a clear container, flower stems become a pleasing part of the arrangement. For a festive variation, conceal the stems by filling the container with cranberries or kumquats (see Holiday Bouquet on page 56).

To prepare flowers, use garden shears to cut stems at a clean angle. Then trim the leaves below the water level (decaying leaves will shorten the life of florals). Refresh flowers before arranging by fully submerging them in cool water for 20 minutes.

Less formal than tulips or roses, white ranunculus blossoms verge on pale green and have the charm of a wildflower bouquet in midwinter (opposite).

KALANCHOE

The tiny, bright blossoms of the kalanchoe, or *Crassulaceae*, keep blooming all winter long with minimum care. Like the poinsettia, the kalanchoe begins to flower when the nights grow long. Once in bloom, it prefers four or more hours of direct sunlight. A type of succulent native to Madagascar, the kalanchoe can go a week or two between waterings. But don't neglect it entirely; a plant kept too dry will turn dull in color and drop its flowers prematurely. One of the easiest flowering house plants to care for, the kalanchoe is handsome enough to stand alone or can provide a spicy accent in a varied floral Christmas tablescape.

Corralled behind a miniature picket fence, fiery little blossoms of the kalanchoe brighten a windowsill (opposite).

In holiday decorating, interesting containers are as important as the plants they hold, adding to the overall design of a Christmas display. If you have a particularly handsome collection of urns, buckets, or pots, create a scene by grouping them and filling them with complementary arrangements of the same potted plant, greenery, or flower.

Experiment with containers like wooden boxes, baskets, or even decorative bags (slip a glass jar inside to waterproof) and play with juxtapositions of color, texture, and mood. Look for unexpected places to use flowers: fill a wooden bowl with glass ball ornaments and potted blooming plants or clip the blooms and tuck them into the Christmas tree, using individual floral vials to keep them fresh.

PAPERWHITES

Most garden centers carry such bulbs as paperwhite narcissus, which have been precooled for forcing. The bulbs grow in either potting soil or pebbles, the latter being best for shallow containers. If you are using soil, choose a container that is twice as deep as a bulb and plant the bulbs an inch apart, with their tops exposed. Place the container in a cool, dark location. Water whenever the soil feels dry to the touch. When the bulbs have developed roots and leaves, move them to a warm, sunny spot. Blooms will usually develop in three to four weeks.

A decorative pot of sprouting bulbs—or just the bulbs themselves—is a welcome holiday gift.

The distinctive sweet fragrance of the paperwhite narcissus has become almost as much a part of Christmas as the scent of pine and cinnamon. With charming clusters of star-shaped blossoms bursting forth on graceful stems, paperwhites have the enchanting purity of a fresh snowfall.

Once in bloom, paperwhites tend to flop. Make a virtue of necessity and tie the tall flowers with colorful ribbon or raffia. Or support the base of the plants by surrounding them with tightly packed naturals, such as berries, fruits, mosses, or greens. Scored, dehydrated oranges, shown opposite, are available in crafts stores.

Opposite: The rough texture of dried pods and oranges contrasts with the delicate blossoms of flowering paperwhites, rooted here in a simple redware dish. Set out fresh bulbs every week or so for a season of continuous blooms.

Above, a stout juniper in a terra-cotta container adorns a painted table in a Maryland hallway. A weathered mantel in Mississippi (opposite) is decorated for the season with privet berries and kumquats tucked among miniature cedar trees in redware pots. Garden centers are good places to look for landscaping plants that can serve as holiday decorations and later be potted or planted outdoors.

MOSS CONTAINER

1 Select an old terra-cotta pot in any size or shape. Gather sheet moss, a hot-glue gun and glue sticks, garden pruners, and assorted pliable twigs with interesting bark or dried pods.

2 Apply glue to the pot and press large sheets of moss in place. Continue gluing moss in this manner to cover the entire pot, over-lapping the top and bottom edges of the moss for a smooth finish.

3 Wrap the lip or the top of the pot with twigs as shown, trimming to fit as necessary; then hot-glue the twigs in place. If your pot is water-tight, fill it with flowers and water as desired. Otherwise, arrange the flowers or the bulbs in a smaller watertight jar and place the jar inside the pot. For top-heavy arrangements, stabilize the pot by par-tially filling it with pebbles or gravel before adding the flowers. For added height, first stuff the pot with old newsprint or craft paper. To secure a small jar in a large container, tuck newsprint or craft paper around the jar inside the pot. If necessary, conceal any unsightly containers or papers with extra moss.

MOSS FORMS

1 Foam comes in a variety of ready-made shapes and sizes. Purchase Styrofoam™ in the desired shapes or cut your own from more pliable florist's foam, which comes in large blocks. To cover the foam shapes, you will need sheet moss, a hot-glue gun and glue sticks, and gold metallic floss.

2 Hot-glue moss sheets to the foam bases to completely cover them, using small pieces to fill in any gaps.

3 Wrap the moss shapes with the floss in patterns. (Ribbons, tiny bead strands, and dried flowers are suitable embellishments, too.) Arrange your finished designs in a bowl or a basket for display or hang them individually as desired.

HOLIDAY BOUQUET

1 Choose a glass container with interesting lines, a pattern, or other detail, considering the effect you want to achieve. We used a footed glass urn, though a footed water glass or even a shot glass will give the same dramatic effect on a smaller scale. Purchase two 8-ounce packages of fresh cranberries for one large arrangement. You'll also need a pitcher of water, garden pruners, and about two dozen fresh roses or other flowers. Select flowers—or simple greens—that complement the red berries.

2 Remove the foliage from the flower stems, using the pruners. (Foliage in water promotes decay and will obstruct the view of the colorful cranberries.) Partially fill the container with berries and arrange flowers at different angles and heights. Fill the container with the remaining berries to just below the rim and then slowly fill the container with water. Replenish water as necessary. Roses will last approximately five to seven days, and cranberries will stay fresh up to three weeks. To keep the berries looking clean, change the water weekly.

Holly

AN ESSAY

erhaps the most ancient of the season's symbols, holly was decking winter halls long before Christmas decorating began. Romans exchanged holly branches during the solstice feast of Saturnalia as a token of goodwill. Druids wore sprigs of holly in their hair in the winter to remind them that the world remained alive even when the sacred oak tree was stripped bare of its leaves. Early Europeans saw in holly's evergreen leaves a promise of the eternal round of seasons and ascribed magical properties to its wood and foliage, believing that spirits chose the holly as their home.

No Christmas scene is complete without a garnish of holly. In nineteenth-century London, street vendors sold holly by the bushel so that Victorian homes could be decorated with the traditional boughs (the Christmas tree, a German tradition, didn't catch on in England until late in the century). English settlers brought their holiday customs with them to America, and holly took root as a Christmas classic.

The holly most identified with Christmas is *Ilex aquifolium,* or English holly, whose glossy, spiked leaves and ruddy berries are an icon of the season. The native American holly, *Ilex opaca,* a handsome but slow-growing variety, was once nearly wiped out by entrepreneurs who harvested the branches to sell at Christmas. Chinese holly *(Ilex cornuta),* a warm-region plant, and Japanese holly *(Ilex crenata),* a cool-region plant, are popular as landscaping shrubs and have fewer spines than English holly.

Hollies come in male and female versions. A female holly will only make berries if it is pollinated by a male holly. If you are growing your own holly, plant one male within 50 feet of every 10 to 20 females for a heavy growth of berries. One notable exception to the male/female rule is the popular Burford holly, a so-called self-fertile variety that produces berries without being pollinated. Burford holly has smooth, nearly spineless leaves and can grow as high as 10 feet.

Sturdy and undemanding, a holly can be left to grow naturally or clipped into a fancy shape (providentially, December is prime time for pruning). Look beyond the more familiar holly varieties to other, more unusual members of the *Ilex* family; over 300 species have been identified around the world. Among the most beautiful hollies is the deciduous winterberry, whose silvery branches and clusters of red fruit brighten the stark winter landscape in cool climates; a recently developed variety bears deep gold berries. Inkberry, an extremely hardy variety, has dark berries, as the name implies, And the long-stalked holly sports cherrylike clusters of berries on long stems.

In today's holiday home, a bit of holly tucked into an arrangement or incorporated into a wreath or a swag adds seasonal sparkle. According to one old tradition, a sprig of holly on the bedpost will invite sweet dreams.

Variegated holly with berries is visually light and airy when made into a traditional wreath (see page 58) or in a swag and a mantel dressing (below). Holly mixes easily with any holiday display, as it does on the antique buffet shown opposite.

FORCING BULBS

1 You will need forcing glasses and hyacinth bulbs. (For glasses and bulb ordering information, see Resources on page 156.) While you can grow hyacinth bulbs in potting soil, colorful forcing glasses are a beautiful alternative. Amaryllis and paperwhite bulbs are traditional forcing choices, too. Just be sure that the forcing glass is heavy enough to support the weight of the larger bulb and bloom of an amaryllis.

2 Fill each glass with water to just below where the bulb will rest (the bulb should not come in contact with the water). Place a bulb right side up in each forcing glass. Put the containers in a cool, dark location until the bulbs develop roots and a short bud; then move them to a warm, sunny spot. Blooming time ranges from three to six weeks. Since blossoms will grow toward the light, rotate the containers periodically to prevent tipping. To ensure blooms throughout the holidays, start forcing bulbs over the course of several weeks in the fall. To prolong the life of bulbs, store them in the refrigerator until you are ready to start forcing.

Mistletoe

he waxy berries and the green leaves of the mistletoe have long been associated with romance and playful flirtation. In ancient times, mistletoe was believed to cure diseases, to provide protection from ghosts and witches, and to bring good luck. Because it grew only in the tops of the tallest trees, it puzzled and fascinated people, who noted that mistletoe flowered in May but did not set its berries until winter. Despite mistletoe's magical reputation, certain varieties of mistletoe berries are toxic and should, therefore, be kept away from pets and small children.

Mistletoe's sticky berries cling to the beaks and the feet of birds, who transport the berries from tree to tree. It establishes its roots high in the branches of a host tree (most commonly, apple, poplar, linden, willow, and oak), from which it draws its water and nutrients. A tree with too luxuriant a growth of mistletoe will eventually weaken and die.

Mistletoe has a long history. Druids began their solstice celebrations by harvesting mistletoe branches with golden knives and by making a strong potion,

suspected to be an aphrodisiac, from its berries. According to Norse legend, mistletoe was sacred to Frigga, the goddess of love. In order to safeguard her son Balder, Frigga asked every animal and plant to promise that nothing that grew on or under the earth would harm him. Her enemy Loki fashioned an arrow from a branch of mistletoe and killed Balder. When Frigga was finally able to restore her son to life, it is said that her tears of joy became the mistletoe's pearly berries.

The romantic powers of mistletoe are still recognized today. Once banned from Christian churches because of its association with pagan rite, mistletoe has become a charming addition to Christmas celebrations. As early as the seventeenth century, English swains were stealing kisses under a sprig of mistletoe. The romantic Victorians popularized the kissing ball, a decorative cluster of mistletoe trimmed with streamers. After each kiss, a berry would be plucked and discarded; when the branch was bare, the kissing would stop. It was a ritual not to be taken lightly: a young woman who stood under a ball and refused a kiss would not marry in the following year.

COLLEC

TIBLES

HOLIDAY KEEPSAKES

THERE WAS A TIME WHEN THAT STUFFED BEAR WAS NEW. Its tan fur was plush, its glass eyes shone, its nose was as black as licorice. The child who unwrapped it on Christmas morning thought it was the most beautiful bear in the world.

Many years and countless happy hours have passed since that Christmas morning, and all that love and use shows. The bear's fur is thin, its jacket is missing, and one ear is torn until barely attached to the head. But once a year the old bear comes down from the attic to sit in the middle of the dining room table, surrounded by greenery and small gifts. It may be battered, it may be worn, but to the child who received it on that long-ago Christmas morning—and to his or her children and grandchildren—it is still the most beautiful bear in the world.

Christmas is a good time to pull out favorite toys or a prized collection, even if the items don't necessarily have a holiday theme. You may be surprised by how comfortably they fit in your seasonal decorating. For instance, cast iron banks lined up on a mantel with sprays of pine and holly become a miniature Christmas town.

Casually grouped teddy bears (above) exude the sweetness of the season. Opposite: A good-natured snowman supervises winter games in a swirling vignette of vintage bisque dolls, arranged on a glass cake stand. A small mirror underneath gives the illusion of a skating pond; a larger mirror behind reflects the fun.

Playthings retired from active duty have a poignant charm that is hard to resist. Keepsakes need not be elaborate or expensive to carry special meaning: Santa figures, snowglobes, and nutcrackers are hardy perennials that never lose their power to please.

Each person brings unique traditions and recollections to the season; these join with decorative holiday remembrances to rekindle warm memories and to connect us with times gone by.

The many faces of Santa Claus appear on such treasures as a decorative light bulb and covered tin buttons from the 1920s (above). Opposite: Felt-clad Santas and Father Christmases date from the 1920s and 1930s; the figure in the blue hat is a Scandinavian Saint Nicholas.

Figures of an adroit juggler and a baby dressed for fun in the snow (top, left) decorate a pair of candy containers made in Germany. Intrepid football heroes in varsity jerseys (bottom, left) are also candy containers and were probably originally designed as party favors. Opposite: Children could pull the rings along the edge of this fanciful barnyard scene and make the figures move; a hidden bellows allowed the animals to "talk." The low-tech ingenuity of vintage toys is part of their charm.

Ankles demurely crossed, an early twentieth-century English doll shows off her holiday finery (above). Twin baby dolls (left) dressed in matching knitted outfits, were made in Germany. Opposite: A rare Izannah Walker doll, made in Rhode Island and patented in 1873, sits on a chest in an upstate New York home. The doll on the right was patented in 1883 by Martha Wellington of Brookline, Massachusetts; the doll on the left is German.

A quizzical painted cat (left) is hung behind a quartet of three-dimensional companions. Rocking horses (below) represent an international stable: the horse on the left, which can be both rocked and pulled, was made in France during the time of Napoleon III; the horse on the far right is also French and is covered with real hide; the painted horse in the background is American and sports a charming landscape panel on its base. Opposite: A playful cotton cat was painted by hand.

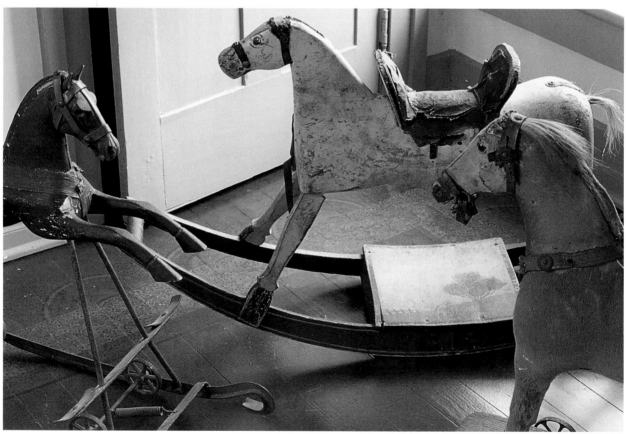

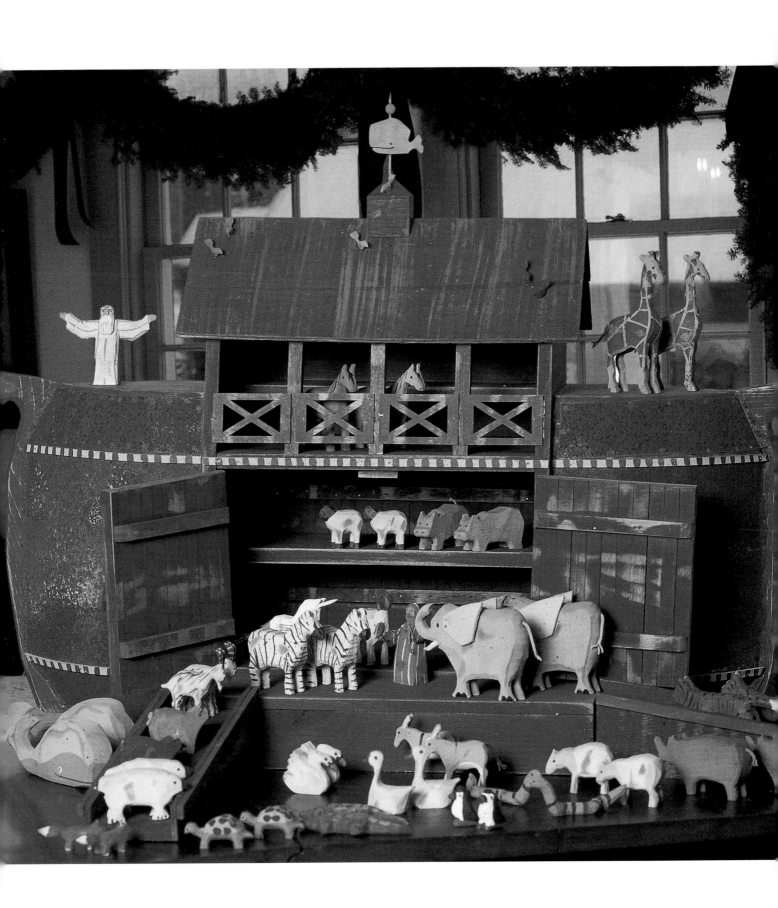

Animals line up two by two (above) in a
Knoxville, Tennessee, home to cele-
brate the season. In Colonial times, a
Noah's ark was often the only plaything
permissible on Sundays. Such a delightful menagerie still holds a special place
in collectors' hearts. Opposite: Barn-
style doors swing wide on a new ark
from Millwood Toys of Ohio. For information on ordering a similar ark, see
Resources on page 156.

Mittens warm the heart as well as the hands. Attached to a line with old-fashioned clothespins, woolen mittens form a winter garland (top, right). Nubby mittens, suspended by twine next to a blanket rack (bottom, right) offer an inventive place to display a bit of Christmas greenery. Opposite: Handmade mittens add to the coziness of a firelit holiday scene.

A row of colorful patchwork stockings (above) hangs from hooks in the family room of an Illinois saltbox. Opposite: An Amish doll fills one of the stockings hung from a dining room peg rail. The stockings were stitched from a salvaged quilt top and embellished with strips of crocheted edging.

Nutcrackers

he stalwart nutcracker, with his bright red coat, fierce eyes, and gigantic teeth, has a proud history. The ancestors of the familiar carved and painted wooden figure first appeared hundreds of years ago in Germany's Erzgebirge Mountains, near the border of the modern Czech Republic. Local tin and silver mine workers supplemented their incomes by carving toys and whimsies; families would assist by assembling and painting the figures. The mines depleted, miners turned to carving full time; peddlers sold their products all over Europe.

German writer E.T.A. Hoffmann visited the Erzgebirge region around 1815 and likely saw the locally made nutcrackers. His fanciful tale of *The Nutcracker and the Mouse King,* with its brave wooden hero, became the basis for Tchaikovsky's ballet *The Nutcracker,* written in 1892. However, the nutcrackers that inspired Hoffmann then would not have resembled the modern red-jacketed figure. Initially, nutcrackers most often represented powerful figures, such as policemen and kings—a bit of gentle social satire since authority figures worked for the common man for a change.

The design we enjoy today dates from 1872, when craftsman Wilhelm Fuechtner created the first wooden soldier nutcrackers. They caught on immediately but only became universally recognized through Tchaikovsky's ballet.

Whimsical figures—representing such local occupations as miner, hunter, fireman, or chimney sweep—also found favor. After World War II, when Americans became avid customers, modern professions were added to the repertoire, with everything from a surgeon to a movie star. Nutcracker collectors are an enthusiastic group, meeting in clubs, traveling to shows, and communicating on-line.

Many craftsmen, including sixth generation Fuechtner family members, still live in the Erzgebirge area. However, the best known German companies, Steinbach and Christian Ulbrecht, relocated to West Germany after World War II, when Erzgebirge became part of East Germany. Inexpensive imports now compete with German nutcrackers, but the most desirable toys are still made by hand, using craftsmanship that has changed little since the Erzgebirge miners carved by firelight in their mountain homes.

TRADITIONS

HOME FOR THE HOLIDAYS. No phrase more poignantly summons up the spirit of the season. From Christmas to New Year's Day, the family circle expands to include friends and neighbors of all generations. Brimming with boisterous good cheer, the holidays become a time to put aside everyday responsibilities and to indulge ourselves in frivolity and sentimentality . . . to make noise, to let our hearts be light, to chase away the chill, and to brighten long nights with laughter.

A week after the Christmas ritual, New Year's Eve is greeted with a raucous clamor. Church bells peal, horns honk, firecrackers pop in the frosty air; inside the house, partygoers make a delightful din with noisemakers, filling the room with a cheerful cacophony as midnight strikes. The New Year safely ushered in, the mood changes as friends join hands to sing "Auld Lang Syne" and then bid each other good night. So the lovely interval between Christmas and New Year's Day ends, as it should, with equal and welcome measures of noise and nostalgia.

Printed tin noisemakers from the 1920s through the 1940s carry cheerful images of clowns and balloons, as well as a whimsical fried-eggs-and-bacon motif (above). Commercial noisemakers are most commonly of a ratchet-, shaker-, or drum-type design. Overleaf: Vintage noisemakers and festive leis await midnight on a bed of juniper trimmings.

CRACKERS

To make a Christmas cracker, place an 8½" by 14½" piece of tissue paper on a slightly larger piece of decorative gift wrap, laid facedown. Center one narrow end of a 5" by 8½" piece of lightweight posterboard along one wide edge of the two papers. Roll the three layers into a tube; secure with glue or tape. Tie off one end with decorative ribbon or cord and fill the tube with trinkets; then tie off the other end. Trim the paper ends with pinking shears. Decorate as desired. A traditional English cracker gets its bang from two strips of chemically treated paper that rub against each other when the cracker is pulled apart. With or without the noise, crackers are a great addition to the holiday table!

Filled with trinkets and a tissue-paper hat, a Christmas cracker does triple duty as a place card, a table decoration, and a party favor (opposite). A traditional delight that dates from Victorian England, crackers are becoming increasingly popular in the United States. For a personal touch, make your own, customizing the crackers with special gifts for guests.

The American Christmas is a melting pot of holiday traditions, a collaboration of the many cultures that make up our own: the German Christmas tree; the hanging stockings, borrowed from the Dutch practice of putting out wooden shoes for presents; the Mexican luminarias that light the way for the infant Jesus on Christmas Eve. It is out of such shared symbols of celebration that each family shapes its own unique rituals. The Christmas cracker, with its sharp "pop" and shower of treats, was a highlight of every Christmas dinner in Victorian England. Invented in the 1840s by a London confectioner, traditional crackers are pure foolish fun—even the grumpiest uncle must don the tissue paper hat that comes inside. Today, these colorful party favors have found their way to modern American Christmas dinner tables.

PAPER HAT

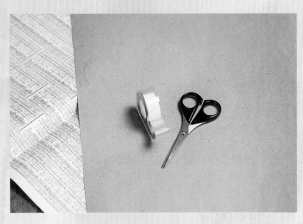

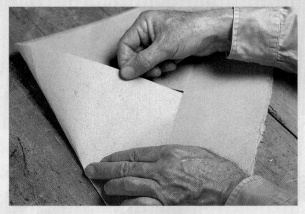

1 To make a party hat, you will need a medium-weight piece of paper and some newsprint for practice, double-stick transparent tape, scissors, and assorted decorative items (optional). To order handmade papers like the one shown here, see Resources on page 156. Or use medium-weight household papers, such as wrapping paper and craft or butcher paper.

2 For each hat, cut a rectangular piece, approximately 20" x 25". Fold the paper in half, with the 20" ends together, and press along the folded edge to make a crease. Unfold the paper and then fold and crease it again, matching the 25" ends. Turn each folded corner toward the center so that they meet, as shown above.

3 Fold up one layer of paper from the open bottom edge and press to make a crease. Turn the folded edge up again to enclose the cut end. Repeat on the opposite side of the hat to finish the brim.

4 On each side, slip a few small pieces of tape between the brim and the hat body to hold the brim in place. Tuck a small piece of evergreen or ribbon or a feather into the brim. Repeat to make as many hats as desired.

CELEBRATION BALLS

1 Layers of crepe paper rolled around decorative balls hide small surprises. Fill the balls with whatever you desire; use them as decorations and then party favors. Once unraveled, they supply small treasures and lots of streamers to enhance any celebration or to remind the recipients of a fun evening.

2 Purchase an assortment of paper fortunes, trinkets, candies, faux jewels, shells, stickers, or minibottles of party bubbles. Check your local variety store for more inexpensive ideas. When selecting the surprises, consider the age of your guests, as these balls make enticing favors for children and adults.

3 You will need small rolls of crepe paper in five to seven bright colors and a small piece of cellophane, both available from party-supply stores.

4 Roll the largest surprise in a square of cellophane. Wind a small roll of crepe paper around the cellophane, shaping it into a ball.

5 Continue in this manner to cover the first treat, winding different colors of crepe paper and tucking small trinkets between the paper layers, until the ball is about the size of a softball.

6 Give the ball a finished look by wrapping it with festive ribbons and thin bands of gold floss. Arrange the finished balls as decorations on a mantel (see page 105) or in a large bowl. Or add a name card and use the balls as place cards to enhance a holiday table.

Deco

RATION

LITTLE THINGS

THE CHRISTMAS SEASON UNFOLDS IN A SERIES of small surprises that are as much a part of the holiday as big events and elaborate celebrations. By the same token, Christmas decorating takes on an added dimension when small touches produce grand effects. Decorations no more complex than a sprig of greenery and a couple of brightly wrapped packages tucked into a corner shelf—or a child's wagon filled with flowering bulbs parked by the front door—remind us to savor each of the passing moments of the holidays.

One of the easiest approaches to Christmas decorating is to pull together contrasting elements: the rough with the smooth, the sophisticated with the homespun. Even everyday objects can have big impact. Try hanging crystal prisms from a birch branch, for instance, or massing vintage snowglobes on a painted tray. Suspend silvery Christmas tree balls from the dining room chandelier, fill a tall hurricane globe with lemons and pears, or charm guests in the kitchen with a tabletop tree trimmed with measuring spoons and cookie cutters.

Surrounded by juniper sprigs and dried seedpods, an antique lantern (above) shines a welcome in a wall niche of a Santa Fe home. Opposite: A weathered plant stand becomes a makeshift Christmas tree when decorated with glass balls and salvaged bird's nests, some of which are displayed on Chinese celadon plates. The window is dressed with Fraser fir.

A casual garden-style arrangement surrounds a rustic birdhouse (above). The house is newly crafted of recycled boards by a New York state artisan. For ordering information, see Resources on page 156. Opposite: French tulips blend with the warm tones of handmade earthenware nativity figures from Guatemala.

Decorations do not have to have a holiday theme to be festive: pull together collections by color, by materials, or by category and then embellish with greenery to create a seasonal vignette. Search seldom-opened drawers and the backs of closets for small treasures—a vase, a pair of hand-knit mittens, some pretty silver bowls.

Mix new merriment with tradition by rethinking your usual displays for a result that is refreshingly contemporary. Celebrations come to life with decorations you had a hand in making.

ILLUMINATIONS

STARS SHINE BRIGHTLY IN THE FROSTY MIDWINTER SKY. Indoors, flickering flames create the shadows of a long winter's night. From a cheerful fire in the hearth to strings of tiny lights twinkling among the branches of the Christmas tree, the holidays have always been celebrated as a festival of lights.

There is no simpler way to convey warmth in your own home than with the glow of candles. Even a single candle casts a flattering and inviting light; a group of candles on a table or on a mantel becomes an instant focal point for holiday decorations. These days, candles come in all scents, colors, shapes, and sizes, from tiny tea lights to slender tapers to chunky pillars. With the variety of candles available, it is easy to dress every room in the house with flattering candlelight. Try various placements for different visual effects: suspend votives from a rustic chandelier or place candles in front of a mirror or next to a bowl of mercury balls to double their reflective power. Add light and warmth to a nonworking fireplace with an arrangement of pillar candles. Light a candle, and a room is transformed.

Sunlight streams through translucent hand-rolled tapers clustered in a pottery planter (above). Opposite: Votive candles shine among pressed glass goblets, vintage linens, and antique Mason's ironstone. Glass candy dishes filled with oversize gumdrops are an inventive and inviting table decoration.

In the courtyard window of a New Mexico home, candle flames highlight the colorful chili peppers strung above (right). Opposite: Inside the house, firelight and candle-light provide all the illumina-tion needed for a cozy holiday scene. On the mantel, votives alternate with piñon branches and crepe-paper celebration balls (see page 94); a hand-painted native American drum provides local flavor. At the table, more sprigs of piñon and tiny peppers decorate a hand-forged candelabra (see Resources on page 156).

Each room offers new possibilities for candle displays. Take a fresh look around and then put your imagination to work.

Purchase quality dripless candles. Although initially more expen-sive than some candles, they last longer and burn with a cleaner flame (this means no wax puddles to clean up later). And always keep safety in mind: arrange candles away from greens and curtains or other fabric, make sure that a candle is secure in its holder, and never leave lighted candles unattended. Using a snuffer to extinguish the flame is always best, as blowing on the flame can spray melted wax onto furnishings and floors.

A pair of seeded eucalyptus and pepper-
berry wreaths are stacked on an iron urn for
a candle centerpiece (above). Opposite:
Pepper berries surround a pillar candle
lowered into a glass urn. Christmas ornaments in muted metallics blend with a
Navajo blanket turned tablecloth.

Votive holders in jewel tones (above) light up
a kitchen table set for a late afternoon snack;
a floor candelabra outside illuminates the
porch. Tapers shed their light from a
traditional punched-tin chandelier. Opposite:
Handmade candles rolled in dried flowers
and herbs line the stairs in a saltbox house.

HANDMADE HOLIDAY

HOMEMADE GIFTS AND DECORATIONS don't need to be complicated or time consuming to reward both the giver and the receiver. There is satisfaction in creating even the simplest item by hand. In fact, the holiday season brings a gift of its own: a reason to indulge creative urges that often get swept aside in the hurry of daily routine.

Handmade presents spread the joy of the season in more ways than one. Simple table decorations, such as the diminutive felt trees shown here, can go home with guests at the end of the meal as party favors; dried herbs and greens bound into a traditional smudge stick (see page 118) serve as a place-card holder for a holiday party and then carry fragrance and good wishes into a friend's home. Homemade decorations can become part of the ongoing Christmas celebration, created each year to be shared with family and friends. The sentiment and care that go into personalizing a table, a gift, or a decoration last long after the holidays. Share the timeless ritual of a handmade Christmas with those you love.

Felt Christmas trees stand on cinnamon-stick trunks and are placed at each setting for a festive miniature forest; silver-leafed clay pots and stars add sparkle. Opposite: the table is dressed with two-tone felt table mats. See the following pages for instructions for the trees and mats.

FELT PLACE MATS

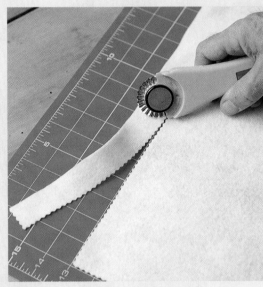

1 To craft these two-tone felt mats, you will need scissors, red and white felt, a cutting mat, a rotary cutter with wide- and small-tooth blades, a ruler, straight pins, red embroidery floss, and a sewing needle. (To make this project completely no-sew, use iron-on fusible tape between the felt layers as a substitute for the embroidery floss.) For a set of six mats, you will need 1 yard of 72"-wide felt in each color. (For craft and cutting supplies, see Resources on page 156.)

2 Using the scissors, cut the red felt into six 14" x 19" rectangles and the white felt into six 13" x 18" rectangles. Using the rotary cutter fitted with the wide-tooth blade and the ruler as a guide, scallop the edges of the red felt rectangles, trimming each mat to 13" x 18". Using the rotary cutter fitted with the small-tooth blade, cut the edges of the white felt rectangles, trimming each mat to 12" x 17".

3 Center one white rectangle on top of each red rectangle and pin them together. With the needle and the red floss, stitch each pair together, using French knots. Place the knots ½" in from the corners and the center top and bottom as shown. (See the French-knot diagrams on page 158.) Remove the pins.

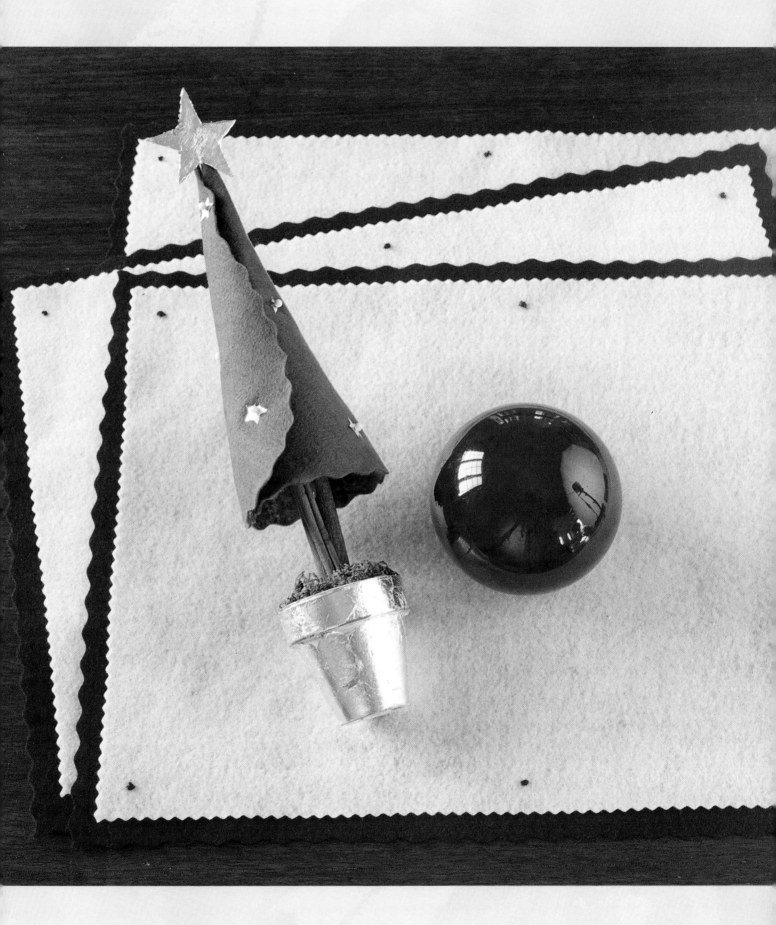

FELT TREES

1 You will need scissors, tracing paper, a cutting mat, a rotary cutter fitted with a wide-tooth blade, a water-soluble marker, lightweight cardboard, a small paintbrush, Mod Podge or white glue and water, Dutch Metal imitation silver leaf, a hot-glue gun and glue sticks, decorator sheet moss, white-headed straight pins, silver sequin stars, and large-headed straight pins. For each tree, you will need one 9" x 12" green felt square, one 5" Styrofoam™ cone, one Styrofoam™ wedge, one 2½"- to 3"-diameter clay pot, and three 4" to 5" cinnamon sticks.

2 Trace and cut out the tree pattern from page 158. Transfer the pattern onto the felt the desired number of times, using the water-soluble marker. Cut out each tree, using the scissors along the straight edge and the rotary cutter along the rounded edges. Set the trees aside.

3 To make the silvered pots and the stars, trace and cut out the star pattern from page 158. Transfer the pattern onto the cardboard, one for each tree; cut them out. With the paintbrush, apply Mod Podge (or a solution of white glue and water) to the surface of the cardboard pieces and each flowerpot. While still tacky, adhere silver leaf. Place a small wedge of foam into each silvered pot and insert the cinnamon sticks into the foam to form a tree trunk. Press one foam cone on top of each cinnamon-stick trunk. Secure the cinnamon stick in the foam with hot glue. Fill the pot with moss.

4 With the scissors, cut off approximately 1" from the cone tip. Wrap each cone with felt, securing with white-headed pins pressed through sequin stars. To top each tree with a cardboard star, insert the point of a large-headed pin into an edge of the star. Then insert the head of the pin into the top of the cone.

PAPER CONES

1 To create a paper cone, purchase or gather hand-made papers in assorted colors and textures. (For ordering information on handmade papers, see Resources on page 156.) You'll also need scrap paper for a template, scissors, a ruler, a pencil, a jumbo paper clip, and a hot glue-gun and glue sticks or double-stick transparent tape. Remember that the size of your finished cone is determined by the size of the paper you begin with. We used an 11" x 17" sheet, though smaller and larger sheets will work nicely, too. Consider the cone's intended contents when determining the size.

2 To make a template, mark off 1" at the center top of the template paper and ½" at the bottom edges, as shown. Draw a line connecting the points to form a large triangle. Fold the outer corners toward the center of the paper along the marked lines and press to make a crease. Place this template on top of a decorative sheet and use it as a guide, folding along creased lines.

3 Once the paper is folded into a large triangle, roll it into a cone. Slip a paper clip over the top edges to maintain the cone shape. Run hot glue or tape along the back seam to secure.

4 Add a decorative band or border of contrasting paper. Using the rotary cutter, cut strips from paper in varying widths. Glue or tape the strips around the top edge of the cone, trimming to fit as needed. Remove the paper clip and fill the cone with small treats.

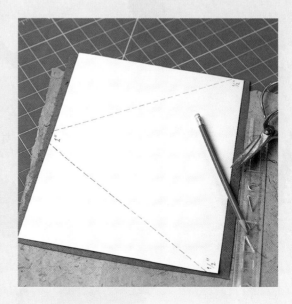

SMUDGE STICKS

1 Smudge sticks are made by binding together natural tree and shrub clippings. Southwestern Native Americans believe that the smoke released from a smoldering smudge stick has purifying and restorative properties. We created these for place cards and favors. To make your own, you will need assorted clippings of piñon, pine, sage, or juniper; colorful twines; garden pruners; and scissors.

2 Trim several short stems of the assorted naturals into 6" to 8" lengths. Unroll a piece of twine long enough to bind the naturals from the top to the bottom. Handling the stems as one, start at the tip of the branches and bind them in a crisscross manner to form a single "stick." Continue wrapping the twine until you reach the base. Then wind the twine tightly around the stems, tie a knot, and clip the excess.

3 To use the smudge stick, light it with a match and gently shake it over a fireproof container to extinguish the flame.

To practice this ancient ritual, which is intended to be relaxing and meditative, slowly move the smudge stick around the perimeter of your body to purify your body and spirit. Then wave the stick toward the north, the south, the east, and the west to honor nature's gifts. To extinguish the stick completely, dip the smoldering end into a shallow dish of water and then place the stick in a fireproof ceramic or metal container. Leave the smudge stick in an open container to dry for reuse. If you plan to give a smudge stick as a party favor or as a small gift, write the directions for use on a small slip of paper and tuck it into a loop of twine wrapped around the smudge stick.

ENTERT

AINING

ORANGE AND
LEMON SLICES

WALNUT SNOWFLAKES

For
The Martins

To You
From Mary

PEANUT BUTTER AND
JELLY SANDWICHES

COOKIES TO GO

A GIFT OF FRAGRANT HOME-BAKED COOKIES warms the heart. When we share the bounty of our kitchen, we also share our affection. Whether we pull out treasured family recipes or experiment with new sweets, we are part of a tradition that stretches back generations . . . and that will be handed on to the next one.

Choose at least one recipe with children in mind. Let them decorate cookies, while you tackle more complicated steps. Kids can also assist with the wrapping (see Pretty Packing on page 135).

If shipping your cookies, plan ahead. Have the baked goods ready three to four weeks before Christmas so that they can be enjoyed during the holidays. Arrange each container in a clean, corrugated box with adequate room for cushioning on all sides. Label the package "perishables" to let the recipient know to open the box right away. A proper send-off ensures that cookies will look and taste as good on arrival as they did right out of the oven. For a personal touch, tuck in a handwritten recipe card.

Biscotti-like Cranberry Pinwheels (above), filled with dried cranberries and cherry preserves, look especially inviting packed in a silver tin lined with waxed tissue paper. Opposite: Walnut Snowflakes fill in a cardboard file box stuffed with wrapping paper.

ORANGE AND LEMON SLICES

THIS DOUGH CAN BE FLAVORED AND
SHAPED INTO ORANGE OR LEMON SLICES.
WE MADE ONE RECIPE OF EACH FOR
PHOTOGRAPHY PURPOSES.

1 cup (2 sticks) butter, softened
½ cup granulated sugar
2 large eggs
1 tablespoon light corn syrup
2 tablespoons orange or lemon extract
3½ cups unsifted all-purpose flour
½ teaspoon salt
2 tablespoons finely grated orange or lemon rind
1 (8-ounce) package coarse sugar crystals (see
    Resources on page 156)
Orange or yellow food coloring
1 teaspoon water

1. In large bowl, with electric mixer on medium speed, beat
butter and sugar until light and fluffy. Beat in 1 egg, the corn
syrup, and orange or lemon extract. Reduce mixer to low;
gradually beat in flour and salt until well mixed. Stir in orange
or lemon rind.

2. If making orange slices, divide dough in half and shape each
into 6-inch-long log. On work surface, flatten 1 side of each
log to resemble the cut side of a half slice of orange. If making
lemon slices, divide dough into quarters and shape each quar-
ter into a 10-inch-long log. Wrap and refrigerate dough 1 hour
or until it is firm enough to slice.

3. Heat oven to 375°F. In 2 small bowls or cups, evenly divide
sugar crystals. Add orange or yellow food coloring to 1 sugar
bowl, a few drops at a time, until desired color is achieved,
leaving other bowl of sugar uncolored. In two more small
bowls, separate remaining egg. Stir water into egg yolk.

4. To make Orange Slices, with sharp knife, cut dough logs
crosswise into ¼-inch-thick slices. Dip rounded edge of orange
slice in yolk mixture to coat, leaving flattened edge of slice
uncoated. Then dip yolk-coated side into orange crystals.
Place cookies, 1 inch apart, on ungreased large baking sheet.
Brush center of cookie with egg white. Sprinkle center with
uncolored sugar crystals. Repeat process with remaining
slices. Bake 10 to 12 minutes or until golden.

5. To make Lemon Slices, with sharp knife, cut logs crosswise
into ¼-inch-thick slices. Dip entire edge of each slice in yolk

mixture and dip into yellow sugar. Place cookies on
ungreased large baking sheet. Brush centers of cookies with
egg white and sprinkle with uncolored sugar crystals. Bake
cookies 8 to 10 minutes or until golden. Transfer cookies to
wire racks immediately and cool completely. Store in an airtight container. Yield: 48 Orange or 80 Lemon Slices.

•NUTRITION INFORMATION PER ORANGE SLICE—PROTEIN: 1 GRAM; FAT: 4 GRAMS;
CARBOHYDRATE: 14 GRAMS; FIBER: .3 GRAM; SODIUM: 58 MILLIGRAMS;
CHOLESTEROL: 19 MILLIGRAMS; CALORIES: 98.

•NUTRITION INFORMATION PER LEMON SLICE—PROTEIN: 1 GRAM; FAT: 2 GRAMS;
CARBOHYDRATE: 8 GRAMS; FIBER: 0; SODIUM: 35 MILLIGRAMS;
CHOLESTEROL: 11 MILLIGRAMS; CALORIES: 59.

WALNUT SNOWFLAKES

A WHITE-CHOCOLATE SNOWFLAKE DESIGN
GIVES THIS WALNUT COOKIE A FESTIVE
WINTRY LOOK.

1 cup (2 sticks) butter, softened
¾ cup confectioners' sugar
2 teaspoons vanilla extract
2 cups unsifted all-purpose flour
1 cup finely chopped walnuts
1 (3-ounce) bar white chocolate, melted

1. In medium-size bowl, with electric mixer on medium
speed, beat butter, sugar, and vanilla until fluffy. Reduce
mixer speed to low; gradually beat in flour until well mixed.
Stir in walnuts.

2. Divide dough in half and shape each half into an 8-inch-
long log. Wrap and refrigerate dough 1 hour or until it is firm
enough to slice.

3. Heat oven to 325°F. Cut each log crosswise into 16 slices.
Place 1 inch apart, on ungreased large baking sheets. Bake 15
to 20 minutes or until lightly browned. Cool cookies 2 minutes on baking sheets; then transfer to wire racks and cool
completely.

4. Place melted chocolate in pastry bag fitted with writing tip
and pipe a snowflake design on each cookie. Cool chocolate
until set. Store in airtight container. Yield: 32 cookies.

•NUTRITION INFORMATION PER COOKIE—PROTEIN: 2 GRAMS; FAT: 9 GRAMS; CARBOHY-
DRATE: 10 GRAMS; FIBER: .5 GRAM; SODIUM: 51 MILLIGRAMS; CHOLESTEROL: 16 MIL-
LIGRAMS; CALORIES: 126.

Peanut Butter and Jelly Sandwiches

THESE MINIATURE SANDWICH-SHAPED COOKIES COMBINE TWO OF CHILDHOOD'S FAVORITE FLAVORS IN A WAY THAT WILL CHARM PBJ LOVERS OF ALL AGES.

¾ cup firmly packed light brown sugar

½ cup (1 stick) butter, softened

⅓ cup chunky peanut butter

1 large egg

1 teaspoon vanilla extract

1½ cups unsifted all-purpose flour

¼ teaspoon baking powder

⅛ teaspoon salt

2 tablespoons grape jelly

1. In medium-size bowl, with electric mixer on medium speed, beat brown sugar, butter, and peanut butter until light and fluffy. Beat in egg and vanilla until well mixed. Reduce mixer speed to low; gradually beat in flour, baking powder, and salt. Gather dough into a ball; form into a 12-inch-long log. With fingers, press dough to resemble a loaf of bread by making top round and squaring off bottom. Wrap and refrigerate dough several hours or until firm enough to slice.

2. Heat oven to 350°F. Lightly grease 2 baking sheets. With sharp knife, cut dough crosswise into ¼-inch-thick slices. Place slices, 1 inch apart, on greased baking sheets. If necessary, reshape cookie slices slightly by hand to resemble small slices of bread.

3. Bake cookies 8 to 10 minutes or until just golden at edges. Cool cookies 2 minutes on baking sheets; then transfer to wire racks and cool completely.

4. When cookies are cool, turn half upside down on work surface. Spoon ¼ teaspoon grape jelly on each. Top with another cookie, right side up. Gently press cookies together to spread jelly evenly. Store in airtight containers. Yield: 24 sandwich cookies.

•NUTRITION INFORMATION PER SANDWICH COOKIE—PROTEIN: 2 GRAMS; FAT: 6 GRAMS; CARBOHYDRATE: 15 GRAMS; FIBER: .5 GRAM; SODIUM: 75 MILLIGRAMS; CHOLESTEROL: 19 MILLIGRAMS; CALORIES: 116.

Cranberry Pinwheels

FILLED WITH SWEET CHERRY AND TART CRANBERRY FLAVORS, THESE COOKIES ARE BAKED TWICE LIKE BISCOTTI.

⅔ cup dried cranberries

½ cup cherry preserves

½ teaspoon ground cinnamon

2¼ cups unsifted all-purpose flour

¾ teaspoon baking powder

¼ teaspoon salt

⅔ cup sugar

½ cup (1 stick) butter, softened

2 large eggs

1 teaspoon vanilla extract

1. In food processor fitted with chopping blade, process cranberries, preserves, and cinnamon 1 minute or until finely chopped; set aside.

2. Heat oven to 325°F. Generously grease and flour large baking sheet. In small bowl, combine flour, baking powder, and salt; set aside.

3. In large bowl, with electric mixer on medium speed, beat sugar and butter until light and fluffy. Beat in eggs and vanilla. Reduce mixer speed to low; gradually beat in flour mixture until well mixed.

4. Divide dough in half. On floured surface, roll half of dough to a 12- by 8-inch rectangle. Evenly spread half of cranberry mixture over dough. Roll up dough lengthwise to form an 8-inch-long log. Repeat with remaining half of dough and cranberry mixture. Place logs, seam side down and 4 inches apart, on prepared baking sheet.

5. Bake logs 30 to 35 minutes or until lightly browned. Cool logs on baking sheet 5 minutes. Carefully transfer logs to cutting board. Using serrated knife and a sawing motion, cut each log diagonally into ½-inch-thick slices. Place slices upright, about ½ inch apart, on baking sheet. Bake 15 minutes longer to dry slices. Transfer slices immediately to wire rack and cool completely. Store cooled cookies in airtight containers. Yield: 32 cookies.

•NUTRITION INFORMATION PER COOKIE—PROTEIN: 2 GRAMS; FAT: 3 GRAMS; CARBOHYDRATE: 17 GRAMS; FIBER: .5 GRAMS; SODIUM: 54 MILLIGRAMS; CHOLESTEROL: 21 MILLIGRAMS; CALORIES: 100.

PRESSED SHORTBREAD

CHOCOLATE-CHIP
SHORTBREAD

Recipe For *Kathrine*
From *Joanne*
Serves *32*   Date *December*

Pressed Shortbread

CERAMIC COOKIE STAMPS, USED HERE TO DECORATE THESE RICH COOKIES, ARE AVAILABLE AT CRAFTS AND HOUSEWARES STORES. SEE RESOURCES ON PAGE 156 FOR INFORMATION ON PURCHASING COOKIE STAMPS BY MAIL.

1 cup (2 sticks) butter, softened
½ cup granulated sugar
⅛ teaspoon salt
2 cups unsifted all-purpose flour
Corn syrup (optional)
Colored sugars (optional)

1. Heat oven to 300°F. Lightly grease 2 baking sheets.

2. In medium-size bowl, with electric mixer on medium speed, beat butter, sugar, and salt until very light and fluffy. Reduce mixer speed to low; add flour, ½ cup at a time, beating until mixture is smooth and silky in appearance.

3. Place ceramic cookie stamps in baking pan and warm in oven 3 minutes; brush with vegetable oil. Between hands, roll slightly rounded measuring teaspoonfuls of dough into 1¼-inch balls. Place on greased baking sheets, 1 inch apart, and press immediately with warm stamp. If stamps cool down, return to oven for a few minutes.

4. Bake cookies 15 to 18 minutes or until just golden at edges. Cool cookies 2 minutes on baking sheets; then transfer to wire racks and cool completely.

5. Before serving, brush designs with corn syrup and sprinkle with colored sugars, if desired. Yield: 36 cookies.

•NUTRITION INFORMATION PER COOKIE WITHOUT CORN SYRUP AND COLORED SUGAR—PROTEIN: 8 GRAMS; FAT: 5 GRAMS; CARBOHYDRATE: 8 GRAMS; FIBER: .2 GRAM; SODIUM: 60 MILLIGRAMS; CHOLESTEROL: 14 MILLIGRAMS; CALORIES: 81.

Chocolate-Chip Shortbread

THE NIP OF SEMISWEET CHOCOLATE AND A HINT OF ORANGE GIVE THESE BUTTERY SHORTBREAD GIANTS A WAKE-UP CALL.

2 cups (4 sticks) butter, softened
1 cup confectioners' sugar
4 cups unsifted all-purpose flour
1 teaspoon salt
1 tablespoon grated orange rind
1 cup mini semisweet chocolate chips
Cellophane and ribbon

1. Heat oven to 375°F. In large bowl, with electric mixer on medium speed, beat butter and sugar until light and fluffy. Reduce mixer speed to low; gradually beat in flour, salt, and orange rind until soft dough forms. Stir in chocolate chips until well combined.

2. Divide dough into 12 equal pieces. Place on ungreased baking sheets, 2 inches apart, and with fingers press dough into 4-inch rounds. With knife, score each cookie into quarters. With tines of fork, press around the edge of each cookie.

3. Bake 20 to 25 minutes or until top is lightly browned. Cool cookies 2 minutes on baking sheets; then transfer to wire racks and cool completely. Store in an airtight container.

4. To wrap for giving, place 3 cookies on top of one another. Wrap stack of cookies in cellophane and tie with ribbon. Before serving, break each cookie along scored lines into quarters. Yield: twelve 4-inch cookies.

•NUTRITION INFORMATION PER ¼ COOKIE—PROTEIN: 1 GRAM; FAT: 9 GRAMS; CARBOHYDRATE: 12 GRAMS; FIBER: .4 GRAM; SODIUM: 65 MILLIGRAMS; CHOLESTEROL: 21 MILLIGRAMS; CALORIES: 132.

DRIED-FRUIT BARS

THIS FIBER-RICH BAR COOKIE DRIZZLED
WITH WHITE CHOCOLATE AND STUDDED
WITH DRIED APRICOTS, CRANBERRIES, AND
RAISINS MAKES A THOUGHTFUL AND
WHOLESOME GIFT DURING THE HOLIDAYS.

⅔ cup chopped dried apricot halves
⅔ cup dried cranberries
⅔ cup seedless golden raisins
2¼ cups unsifted all-purpose flour
1 cup sugar
¾ cup old-fashioned rolled oats
1 teaspoon ground cinnamon
½ teaspoon baking soda
½ teaspoon salt
1 cup (2 sticks) butter, melted
1 large egg, lightly beaten
2 teaspoons vanilla extract
6 (1-ounce) squares or bars white chocolate,
   melted

1. Heat oven to 350°F. Grease 13- by 9-inch baking pan. In
small bowl, combine apricots, cranberries, and raisins; set
aside.

2. In medium-size bowl, combine flour, sugar, rolled oats,
cinnamon, soda, and salt. Stir in butter, egg, and vanilla until
mixture resembles coarse crumbs. Press mixture into greased
baking pan.

3. Bake 15 to 20 minutes or until lightly browned. Place pan
on wire rack. Spread melted chocolate evenly over baked oat-
meal layer. Top with dried fruit mixture. Cool completely.
Cut into twenty-four 2¾- by 1½-inch bars. Store in airtight
containers. Yield: 24 bars.

•NUTRITION INFORMATION PER BAR—PROTEIN: 3 GRAMS; FAT: 10 GRAMS;
CARBOHYDRATE: 31 GRAMS; FIBER: 2 GRAMS; SODIUM: 136 MILLIGRAMS;
CHOLESTEROL: 31 MILLIGRAMS; CALORIES: 223.

TOFFEE CUPS

FESTIVE FLUTED PAPER PAN LINERS ADD TO
THE APPEAL OF THESE CRUNCHY TOFFEE-
FILLED BITES.

½ cup granulated sugar
½ cup firmly packed light brown sugar
½ cup (½ stick) vegetable shortening
1 large egg
1 teaspoon vanilla extract
1½ cups unsifted all-purpose flour
½ teaspoon baking soda
½ teaspoon salt
½ cup toffee bits
½ cup chopped hazelnuts
48 large semisweet chocolate chips

1. Heat oven to 325°F. Place forty-eight 1-inch fluted paper
liners in gem pan cups or mini muffins pan.

2. In large bowl, with electric mixer on high speed, beat granulated and brown sugars, shortening, egg, and vanilla until
light and fluffy. Reduce mixer speed to low; gradually beat in
flour, soda, and salt until well mixed. With spoon, stir in toffee bits and hazelnuts.

3. Drop dough by level measuring teaspoonfuls into prepared gem pans or mini muffin pans.

4. Bake cookie cups 8 to 10 minutes or until just golden at
edges. Remove from oven and immediately place 1 chocolate
chip in center of each; gently press chocolate chip to cookie to
adhere. Cool cookies 2 minutes in pans; then transfer to wire
racks and cool completely. Store in airtight containers. Yield:
48 Toffee Cups.

•NUTRITION INFORMATION PER TOFFEE CUP—PROTEIN: .8 GRAM; FAT: 5 GRAMS;
CARBOHYDRATE: 9 GRAMS; FIBER: .3 GRAM; SODIUM: 38 MILLIGRAMS;
CHOLESTEROL: 4 MILLIGRAMS; CALORIES: 79.

CHOCOLATE, COCONUT, AND
PISTACHIO MACAROONS

GINGERBREAD
BOXES

TOFFEE CUPS

DRIED-FRUIT
BARS

Chocolate, Coconut, and Pistachio Macaroons

THESE EASILY ASSEMBLED MACAROONS
NEED EXTRA TIME IN A COOLING OVEN
TO DRY THEM THOROUGHLY.

3 large egg whites, at room temperature
⅛ teaspoon salt
1 cup sugar
6 (1-ounce) squares or bars unsweetened chocolate,
   melted
1 cup sweetened flaked coconut
¾ cup plus 2 tablespoons shelled pistachios, finely
   chopped (see Note)
¼ cup semisweet chocolate chips, melted

1. Heat oven to 350°F. Lightly grease 2 baking sheets.

2. In large bowl, with electric mixer on high speed, beat
whites and salt until frothy. Gradually add sugar, beating until
very light and fluffy—about 5 minutes.

3. Very gently fold chocolate, coconut, and ¾ cup pistachios
into beaten whites. Drop by rounded measuring teaspoonfuls,
1 inch apart, onto greased baking sheets.

4. Bake macaroons 10 to 12 minutes or until just firm. Turn
off oven; leave macaroons in oven with door slightly ajar 30
minutes for interior of cookies to crisp. Transfer to wire racks.
Drizzle melted chocolate chips over tops of macaroons and
sprinkle with remaining 2 tablespoons pistachios; cool completely. Store in airtight containers. Yield: 60 cookies.

Note: Pistachios are available by mail. See Resources on
page 156.   •

Gingerbread Boxes

THESE FESTIVE BOXES CARRY THE AROMA
OF HOLIDAY BAKING WHEREVER THEY GO.
THEY ARE A TASTEFUL WAY TO PACKAGE
AN ASSORTMENT OF COOKIES.

4½ cups unsifted all-purpose flour
2 teaspoons ground cinnamon
2 teaspoons ground ginger
¼ teaspoon ground cloves
¼ teaspoon salt
1 cup (1 stick) vegetable shortening
¾ cup sugar
1 cup dark corn syrup
1 large egg
Paper for patterns
Cardboard for frames
Masking tape
Foil-covered wrapping paper or aluminum foil
Royal Frosting (recipe follows)
Yarn or string
Decorative ribbons

1. In medium-size bowl, combine flour, cinnamon, ginger,
cloves, and salt.

2. In large bowl, with electric mixer on medium speed, beat
shortening and sugar until light and fluffy. Beat in corn syrup
and egg. Reduce speed to low; gradually beat in flour mixture
to make a stiff dough.

3. Wrap dough in plastic wrap and set aside at room temperature while making patterns and cardboard frame pieces—no
longer than 30 minutes.

4. Make patterns for 1 large square box, 1 small square box,
and 1 octagonal box. From paper, draw and cut out a 6- by 4-
inch rectangle for large box sides, a 6- by 2¾-inch rectangle for
small box sides, a 6¼-inch square for box lids, a 4- by 2-inch
rectangle for octagonal box sides, and a 5¼-inch octagon (see
Note on next page) for octagonal box lid.

5. Make cardboard frame pieces: From cardboard, using
paper patterns as a guide, draw and cut out 4 large square box
sides, 4 small square box sides, 2 square box lids, 8 octagonal
box side pieces, and 1 octagonal box lid. In addition, draw and
cut out two 6-inch squares and one 5-inch octagon (see Note)
for box bottoms. Set pieces aside.

6. Heat oven to 350°F. Cover 2 large baking sheets with aluminum foil. On prepared sheets, roll out one third of gingerbread dough to ⅛-inch thickness. Using paper patterns as a guide, cut out 4 large square box sides, 4 small square box sides, 2 square box lids, 8 octagonal box sides, and 1 octagonal box lid, leaving ¼ inch between pieces. If desired, using small cookie cutters (see Resources on page 156) or a kitchen knife, score designs into dough, or cut out shapes from dough scraps and place on box pieces to decorate.

7. Bake gingerbread pieces 12 to 15 minutes or until firm and golden brown. While gingerbread is still warm, measure 2 of each size square box sides against patterns and trim off excess caused by expansion during baking. On remaining box sides, trim only from bottom to match pattern, allowing excess on side of pieces to remain. Select and set aside 1 of each size for fronts of square boxes. For backs of square boxes, from remaining pieces of each size, trim an additional ¼ inch from bottom to allow room for lid to open. Repeat until all pieces have been baked. Cool pieces on flat surface.

8. Meanwhile, assemble cardboard frames: On work surface, place the four 6- by 4-inch cardboard rectangles side by side with 4-inch edges touching. Tape pieces securely together. Shape pieces into a box and tape together remaining edge. Tape bottom securely to box; tape only 1 edge of lid onto box. Repeat with remaining pieces to make small square box and octagonal box. Do not tape lid onto octagonal box. Line insides of boxes and cover bottoms of lids with foil wrapping paper or aluminum foil, extending and folding lining ½ inch over edge and onto outside of boxes. Tape into place.

9. Prepare Royal Frosting. Spread some frosting on outside of 1 cardboard box. Press gingerbread side pieces onto box. Tie a piece of yarn or string around boxes to hold gingerbread in place until secure. Frost cardboard top of box; press gingerbread top in place. Repeat with remaining 2 boxes. Set aside at least 3 hours to dry.

10. When boxes are dry, remove yarn; decorate with ribbons. Store in airtight containers until ready to fill. Yield: 3 boxes.

ROYAL FROSTING:

In medium-size bowl, combine 1 pound confectioners' sugar, 3 tablespoons meringue powder (see Resources on page 156), and ¼ cup plus 2 tablespoons cold water. With electric mixer on high speed, beat until thick and fluffy. Cover tightly with a damp towel while using to keep from drying out.

Note: To make octagon patterns from paper, draw and cut out a 5-inch square. Fold square into eighths so that all folds radiate from center. On longer folded side, measure and mark a spot 2½ inches from point of triangular piece (center of folded square). Draw and cut a line from that dot to the end of the shorter folded side. Open for 5-inch octagon. For 5¼-inch octagon, trace 5-inch pattern and cut ⅛ inch larger on all sides.

BLACK-AND-WHITE PECAN BLONDIES

THE CUT EDGES OF THESE BUTTERY PECAN TRIANGLES ARE SEALED WITH WHITE AND DARK FROSTING TO KEEP THEM FROM DRYING OUT.

1½ cups firmly packed light brown sugar
½ cup (1 stick) butter, softened
2 large eggs
2 teaspoons vanilla extract
1½ cups unsifted all-purpose flour
1 teaspoon baking powder
½ teaspoon salt
1 cup coarsely chopped pecans
Black and White Frosting (recipe follows)
48 pecan halves

1. Heat oven to 350°F. Lightly grease 13- by 9-inch baking pan.

2. In medium-size bowl, with electric mixer on medium speed, beat brown sugar and butter until light and fluffy. Beat in eggs and vanilla until well mixed. Reduce mixer speed to low; beat in flour, baking powder, and salt until well mixed. With rubber spatula, stir in pecans; spread dough evenly in greased baking pan.

3. Bake blondies 15 to 18 minutes or until just golden at edges. Cool blondies 5 minutes in baking pan; then cut into 24 rectangles. Cut rectangles diagonally in half to make 48 triangles. Transfer blondies from pan to wire racks and cool completely.

4. Meanwhile, prepare Black and White Frosting. When blondies are cool, with small spatula, frost half of each with white frosting. Allow to dry on wire racks until frosting is firm enough to be touched—about 30 minutes. Frost remaining half of each blondie with cocoa frosting and top with pecan half. Set blondies aside until completely dry—about 1 hour. Store between sheets of waxed paper in an airtight container. Yield: 48 blondies.

BLACK AND WHITE FROSTING:

In medium-size bowl, with fork, stir together 1 pound confectioners' sugar, ¼ teaspoon salt, and 2 to 4 teaspoons water until thin frosting forms. Transfer half of frosting to small bowl and stir in 2 tablespoons unsweetened cocoa powder and 1 to 2 teaspoons additional water until combined. Cover and set aside.

•NUTRITION INFORMATION PER BLONDIE—PROTEIN: 1 GRAM; FAT: 5 GRAMS; CARBOHYDRATE: 20 GRAMS; FIBER: .4 GRAM; SODIUM: 65 MILLIGRAMS; CHOLESTEROL: 14 MILLIGRAMS; CALORIES: 124.

BLACK-AND-WHITE PECAN BLONDIES

Cinnamon Suns, Moons, and Stars

THESE CELESTIALLY INSPIRED CORNMEAL
COOKIES ARE EASY TO SHAPE BY HAND
RIGHT ON THE BAKING SHEET. THIS IS A
GOOD RECIPE TO USE WHEN BAKING
WITH CHILDREN.

1½ cups sugar
½ cup (1 stick) butter, softened
½ cup (½ stick) vegetable
   shortening
1 large egg
½ teaspoon vanilla extract
1½ cups unsifted all-purpose flour
¾ cup yellow cornmeal
½ teaspoon baking powder
¼ teaspoon salt
1 tablespoon ground cinnamon

1. Heat oven to 350°F. Lightly grease 2 baking sheets.

2. Reserve ¼ cup sugar in plastic sandwich bag. In medium-
size bowl, with electric mixer on medium speed, beat remaining 1¼ cups sugar, the butter, shortening, egg, and vanilla
until well mixed. Reduce mixer speed to low; gradually beat
in flour, cornmeal, baking powder, and salt until soft dough
forms. Divide dough into 3 equal balls.

3. Stir cinnamon into reserved ¼ cup sugar in plastic bag.
Divide one-third of dough into 24 equal pieces. Between
hands, roll each piece into 1-inch ball. Drop balls, several at a
time, into cinnamon sugar in bag and shake until well coated.
Place cinnamon-sugar-coated balls, 1½ inches apart, on
greased baking sheets and press gently to flatten to ½ inch
thickness to make suns.

4. Bake cookies 12 to 15 minutes or until just golden at edges.
Cool cookies 2 minutes on baking sheets; then transfer to
wire racks and cool completely.

5. Repeat making and coating balls from second third of
dough; shape cinnamon-sugar-coated balls of dough into 2-
inch crescent moons on baking sheets and bake and cool as
directed above.

6. Repeat making, coating, and flattening balls from last
third of dough; pinch flattened balls around edges 5 times to

CINNAMON SUNS,
MOONS, AND STARS

shape into stars. Bake and cool as directed above. Store cookies in airtight containers. Yield: 72 cookies.

•NUTRITION INFORMATION PER COOKIE—PROTEIN: .5 GRAM; FAT: 3 GRAMS;
CARBOHYDRATE: 8 GRAMS; FIBER: .2 GRAM; SODIUM: 118 MILLIGRAMS;
CHOLESTEROL: 6 MILLIGRAMS; CALORIES: 57.

GINGER-MARMALADE
THUMBPRINTS

Ginger–Marmalade Thumbprints

SWEET GINGER MARMALADE AND CHOPPED CANDIED CHERRIES PERK UP THESE CLASSIC COOKIES. WE MADE TWO BATCHES FOR PHOTOGRAPHY, ADDING GREEN CHERRIES TO THE MARMALADE MIXTURE OF ONE AND RED CHERRIES TO THE OTHER.

2 tablespoons ginger marmalade

2 tablespoons chopped green or
   red candied cherries

1 tablespoon finely chopped pecans

2¼ cups unsifted all-purpose flour

½ teaspoon ground nutmeg

¼ teaspoon salt

1 cup (2 sticks) butter, softened

⅔ cup sugar

1 large egg

2 teaspoons vanilla extract

1. Heat oven to 375°F. In small bowl, combine marmalade, cherries, and pecans; set aside. In medium-size bowl, combine flour, nutmeg, and salt; set aside.

2. In large bowl, with electric mixer on medium speed, beat butter and sugar until light and fluffy. Beat in egg and vanilla. Reduce mixer speed to low; gradually beat in flour mixture until well mixed.

3. Measure a scant tablespoon of dough and shape into a ball. Repeat process with remaining dough to make a total of 36 balls. Place balls, 2 inches apart, on ungreased large baking sheets. With thumb, make an indentation in top of each ball of dough. Spoon about ¼ teaspoon marmalade mixture into each indentation.

4. Bake 10 to 12 minutes until edges are lightly browned. Cool cookies 2 minutes on baking sheets; then transfer to wire racks and cool completely. Store in airtight containers. Yield: 36 cookies.

•NUTRITION INFORMATION PER COOKIE—PROTEIN: 1 GRAM; FAT: 5 GRAMS; CARBOHYDRATE: 11 GRAMS; FIBER: .3 GRAM; SODIUM: 60 MILLIGRAMS; CHOLESTEROL: 20 MILLIGRAMS; CALORIES: 97.

Pretty Packing

- Present handmade goods with style in a thoughtfully prepared package. Remember that half the fun of receiving a holiday gift lies in the delicious unveiling. A cleverly turned-out package is an expression of love from the heart of the sender.

- Buy a container with personality. A sleek stainless-steel tin, a classic white baker's carton, a transparent vellum envelope, or a utilitarian cardboard tube—each makes a bold statement all its own. Peruse your local kitchen-supply store or bakery for interesting options.

- Cushion contents beautifully with sophisticated fillers, such as colorful paper shreds, waxed tissues, tinted cellophane, or parchment papers. Pad the container with a few layers before and after you add baked goods. Close the package and gently shake it. If you can hear the contents shifting, add more filler.

- Personalize packages with gift tags. It's a snap to turn plain merchant tags, available from office-supply stores, into something special when you embellish them with wax seals, rubber stamps, or fine ribbons.

VINTAGE TINS

A decorative cookie tin needn't be made of tin, and it needn't have originally held cookies. Any pretty box, as long as it is clean and has not been used earlier for toxic materials, can enhance a gift of cookies. Look through antique stores for printed pasteboard boxes, papier-mâché boxes, inlaid wood boxes, souvenir shell boxes, and old hatboxes. At the higher end of the price scale, look for antique wallpaper-covered boxes, Shaker boxes, tramp art boxes, and document boxes.

Vintage papier-mâché boxes, hand-painted with sprigs of holly, become a charming decoration when tied with ribbon and piled into a basket with fresh greens (opposite). Christmas-themed antiques such as these are popular with collectors but can still be found at reasonable prices.

Decorated commercial advertising tins were first used in the United States in the 1820s and remain a nostalgic favorite today. Once a staple on the shelves of country stores and used to hold everything from biscuits to typewriter ribbons, the colorful tins were saved and recycled by frugal housewives and still turn up regularly at yard sales, antique stores, and auctions. Although old and rare tins sell to collectors for hundreds of dollars, it is easy to find attractive tins of more recent vintage for a fraction of such a cost.

A pretty cookie container can be a gift in itself, especially when tied up in ribbon and embellished with a sprig of greenery. Collect inexpensive baskets, boxes, and tins throughout the year for holiday cookies and make the gifts from your kitchen distinctive.

PANCAKE PERFECTION

FROM DELICATE FRENCH CRÊPES TO STURDY blini, pancakes translate into nearly every culinary language. But there is still something distinctively American about a snowy day, a warm kitchen, and a stack of steaming cakes. Our ancestors prized pancakes for their versatility; easy to cook wherever there is heat and a griddle, they were perfect for a young nation on the move.

Today, we still love pancakes. Fragrant, nostalgic, filling, and tasty, pancakes are a good choice for a houseful of holiday guests. Ready in minutes, pancakes can be served in an endless stream or stacked in a warm oven for late risers. Although there are plenty of mixes on the market, pancakes are easy to make from scratch and well worth the effort. Pancakes can be varied in many ways by altering their ingredients just a bit. Taste and texture change dramatically, depending on whether you use white flour, buckwheat flour, cornmeal, or some other kind of flour or meal. Extras, such as blueberries or diced apples, fruit toppings, and syrups, take the pancake far beyond its humble roots.

A jumbo stack of Whole-Wheat Granola, Buckwheat-Banana, and Cornmeal-Blueberry pancakes (above), topped with Apricot Cranberry Sauce, are cut into layered wedges so that guests can sample all three. Opposite: A Paul Bunyan-sized serving of Buttermilk Flapjacks satisfies holiday hunger. See the following pages for recipes.

BUTTERMILK FLAPJACKS

IF YOU'RE MAKING A STACK, KEEP THE FINISHED FLAPJACKS WARM IN A 200°F OVEN WHILE COOKING THE REMAINING BATTER. WE MADE SEVERAL BATCHES FOR THE PHOTOGRAPH.

2 cups unsifted all-purpose flour
1 tablespoon sugar
½ teaspoon salt
2¼ cups buttermilk
1½ teaspoons baking soda
2 large eggs, lightly beaten
2 tablespoons butter, melted
Vegetable oil for frying
Butter or margarine
Maple syrup
Fresh strawberries and blueberries (optional)

1. In large bowl, combine flour, sugar, and salt. In a small bowl or glass measuring cup, combine buttermilk and baking soda. Immediately add buttermilk mixture, eggs, and melted butter to flour mixture. Stir just until dry ingredients are moistened. (Mixture should be lumpy.)

2. Lightly oil a griddle or 8-inch skillet and heat over medium heat. Spread a heaping ½ cup of batter on griddle to make a 6-inch flapjack. Cook until bubbles form and begin to break on top of surface; turn flapjack over and cook until bottom is golden brown. Remove flapjack and serve immediately or place on a baking sheet in 200°F. oven to keep warm until all flapjacks are done.

3. Repeat with remaining batter, adding more oil to pan as necessary. Serve flapjacks warm with butter, maple syrup, and strawberries and blueberries, if desired. Yield: six 6-inch flapjacks.

NUTRITIONAL INFORMATION PER FLAPJACK WITH 1 TEASPOON BUTTER AND 2 TABLE-SPOONS MAPLE SYRUP (NO FRUIT)—PROTEIN: 10 GRAMS; CARBOHYDRATE: 64 GRAMS; FAT: 10 GRAMS; FIBER: 1 GRAM; SODIUM: 573 MILLIGRAMS; CHOLESTEROL: 93 MILLIGRAMS; CALORIES: 389.

GIANT PANCAKES

TO SERVE A CROWD, PREPARE THE RECIPE WITH ITS THREE PANCAKE VARIATIONS AND STACK THEM AS WE HAVE DONE. BUT DON'T LET THE SIZE OF THIS RECIPE STOP YOU FROM MAKING ONLY ONE VARIETY.

Whole-Wheat Granola Batter (recipe follows)
Vegetable shortening or oil for frying
Buckwheat-Banana Batter (recipe follows)
Cornmeal-Blueberry Batter (recipe follows)
Apricot Cranberry Sauce (recipe follows)
Irish Bacon, cooked (optional, see Note)
Sausage links, cooked (optional)

1. Prepare Whole-Wheat Granola Batter. Heat a nonstick 10-inch skillet over low heat; generously brush with shortening to coat. Spoon half of batter into skillet and with a large pancake turner, spread batter evenly. Cover skillet and cook until bottom of pancake is light brown and top surface looks dry—about 5 minutes. Meanwhile, heat oven to 375°F. With vegetable shortening, generously grease 11-inch rounds in the centers of 2 baking sheets.

2. With the pancake turner, loosen pancake; invert onto center of one greased baking sheet. Bake pancake 5 minutes or until bottom is golden brown. Meanwhile, brush skillet with more shortening; add remaining half of batter and repeat to make second pancake.

3. When granola pancakes are baked, remove from baking sheets to 2 wire racks; then prepare Buckwheat-Banana Batter into pancakes using same method. When buckwheat pancakes are baked, place one on top of each granola pancake. Repeat to make Cornmeal-Blueberry Batter into pancakes; place one on top of each buckwheat pancake.

4. To assemble Giant Pancake stack, on an ovenproof serving platter, place one stack of pancakes on top of the other to make six layers. Place in oven 5 minutes to heat until warm. To serve, cut into 8 wedges and top with Apricot Cranberry Sauce. Serve with Irish bacon and sausage links, if desired. Yield: 8 servings.

WHOLE-WHEAT GRANOLA BATTER:

In large bowl, combine 1 cup unsifted all-purpose flour, ¾ cup whole-wheat flour, ¾ cup unsweetened granola (or ½ cup

TOPPING IT OFF

Make your pancakes gourmet with a fruit topping, such as the Apricot Cranberry Sauce shown here (recipe below). And for the fruit-lover, here's another option that is short on ingredients but big on taste. You'll need about 16 ounces of your favorite frozen berries. Thaw and drain the berries, reserving the juice. Mix the juice, ½ cup of water, 1 tablespoon plus 1 teaspoon cornstarch, and 3 tablespoons of sugar in a saucepan. Cook over low heat about 5 minutes. Add the berries, cover, and cook 5 minutes. Stir in 1 tablespoon of lemon juice. Serve warm.

old-fashioned rolled oats plus ¼ cup dark seedless raisins), 4 teaspoons baking powder, 1 tablespoon sugar, and ¼ teaspoon salt. Stir in 1¼ cups milk, 1 large egg, lightly beaten, and 2 tablespoons vegetable oil, just until combined.

BUCKWHEAT-BANANA BATTER:

Prepare Whole-Wheat Granola Batter, substituting ¾ cup buckwheat flour for the whole-wheat flour and 2 small bananas, sliced, for the granola.

CORNMEAL-BLUEBERRY BATTER:

Prepare Whole-Wheat Granola batter, substituting 1 cup cornmeal for the whole-wheat flour and ¾ cup blueberries for the granola.

Note: Irish bacon is available by mail. See Resources on page 156.

NUTRITIONAL INFORMATION PER SERVING WITHOUT APRICOT CRANBERRY SAUCE, BACON, OR SAUSAGE—PROTEIN: 17 GRAMS; FAT: 24 GRAMS; CARBOHYDRATE: 87 GRAMS; FIBER: 7 GRAMS; SODIUM: 779 MILLIGRAMS; CHOLESTEROL: 94 MILLIGRAMS; CALORIES: 619.

APRICOT CRANBERRY SAUCE

SWEET AND TANGY, THIS APRICOT SAUCE IS THE PERFECT COMPLEMENT TO OUR STACK OF GIANT PANCAKES.

⅔ cup chopped dried apricot halves
1 cup apricot preserves
1 cup water
2 tablespoons chopped cranberries
1 tablespoon lemon juice

1. In small saucepan, place apricots and enough water to cover by ½ inch; heat to simmer and cook, uncovered, 40 to 45 minutes or until about 2 tablespoons liquid remain and apricots are very tender. Transfer apricots with liquid to blender and puree.

2. Return apricot puree to same saucepan. Add preserves, water, and cranberries and heat over low heat. Cook, stirring to melt preserves and blend mixture. Remove from heat; stir in lemon juice and serve. Yield: 2½ cups.

NUTRITIONAL INFORMATION PER ¼ CUP—PROTEIN: .5 GRAM; FAT: .01 GRAM; CARBOHYDRATE: 28 GRAMS; FIBER: 1 GRAM; SODIUM: 4 MILLIGRAMS; CHOLESTEROL: 0 MILLIGRAM; CALORIES: 108.

DRESSING THE TABLE

THERE ONCE WAS A TIME when a hostess was loathe to serve her guests on mismatched china or silver. It was a clear indication that she had to borrow plates and spoons from the neighbors. Today, we mix and match with pride, showing off favorite pieces and using the antique next to the new.

  Although the old rules have long since been broken, the most pleasing tablescapes still follow some basic design principles. The table goes together easily if you have a unifying theme—for instance, color, shape, or a family of patterns (such as a table set with several patterns of floral china)—and if you keep the items in proportion. Once you've decided on a theme, mix with freedom: create a place setting with silver plate (still a bargain at flea markets) and heirloom sterling, or with fine porcelain and chunky earthenware. Good combinations include more than two of one style and, ironically, look balanced with uneven numbers. Show off your favorite serving pieces, too. When in doubt, use it.

A carefully edited palette of cream and white binds together a variety of creamware and porcelain (above). Opposite: No two utensils are the same (even the monograms are different) but the blend of sterling, silver plate, and bone-handled tableware makes a rich mix.

Five forks with five patterns, but they look beautiful together because they share slender lines and a nod to tradition (top, left). Buying by the piece makes it easy to build a collection over time; while complete sets of flatware command high prices at antique stores, individual pieces are often more affordable. Milky white plates in three different patterns (bottom, left) were never intended to be fine tableware, but they look elegant when paired with vintage hemstitched table linens. Opposite: Whites and neutrals, brought together in a single table setting, are a year-round palette that looks particularly serene at Christmas. Bone-handled knives, such as the ones shown here, should always be washed and dried by hand.

CHRISTMAS DINNER

CHRISTMAS DINNER PUTS THE FESTIVE CAP ON A long day of fun and sharing. But to a time-starved cook contemplating a table of hungry guests, the holiday feast can be a daunting challenge. One way to minimize stress in the kitchen is to plan the menu around dishes that can be made ahead or that don't require precious oven or refrigerator space. The succulent turkey shown opposite, for instance, was marinated in apple juice and sage and then smoked on an outdoor grill, leaving the oven free for warming other dishes.

But Christmas dinner is far more than a menu. The people gathered around the dining room table make the meal memorable, and the small rituals repeated each year are some of the threads that bind families together. On Christmas Day, family and guests still linger at the table, reminiscing, making plans for the New Year, or retelling a favorite family story. The preparation is done, and even the cook can relax as the talk carries on and the candles burn lower in their holders.

Menu

Apple-Sage Marinated Smoked Turkey

Caesar Salad with Parmesan Crisps

Braised Onions, Carrots and Brussels Sprouts

Corn and Pepper Stuffing

Twice-Baked Potatoes

Raisin Fennel Rolls

Cranberry Orange Compote

Pear Apricot Cobbler

APPLE-SAGE MARINATED SMOKED TURKEY

A SWEETENED BRINE OF APPLE JUICE, WATER, VINEGAR, SAGE, AND SALT GIVES THIS TURKEY FLAVOR AND SUCCULENCE WHEN IT'S SMOKED IN A COVERED CHARCOAL OR GAS GRILL.

MAKES 12 SERVINGS

2 (12-ounce) cans frozen apple juice concentrate, thawed

4 (12-ounce) cans cold water—use apple juice can to measure

½ cup cider vinegar

½ cup fresh sage leaves, chopped, or 3 tablespoons crumbled dried sage

¼ cup pickling salt

½ teaspoon dried crushed red pepper

1 (12-pound) fresh or thawed frozen turkey

Gravy (recipe follows)

4 cups small wood chips (apple wood, grapevine cuttings, hickory, or other fruitwood)

2 tablespoons olive oil

1 medium-size baking or cooking apple (Winesap, Rome Beauty, Golden Delicious)

Fresh sage sprigs (optional)

1. In 2-gallon plastic food-storage bag placed in large bowl, combine undiluted apple juice, water, vinegar, sage, salt, and pepper. Set mixture aside.

2. Remove giblets and neck from turkey; rinse, wrap, and refrigerate to make Gravy. Rinse and place turkey, breast side down, in apple-juice mixture. Seal bag and refrigerate turkey for 2 days, turning the bird every 12 hours.

3. About 8 hours before serving, drain turkey, reserving marinade. Place turkey, breast side up, on wire rack in shallow small roasting pan. Refrigerate turkey uncovered for at least 4 hours to dry out skin or until ready to grill. Refrigerate marinade. Meanwhile, using reserved turkey giblets and neck, prepare turkey broth in Gravy recipe.

4. At least 4 hours before serving turkey, soak wood chips in enough water to cover in a container. If using charcoal grill, ignite 40 charcoal briquettes. When briquettes are hot, place equally around a 9-inch square disposable aluminum foil drip

pan placed in center of the charcoal grate in grill. On a gas grill, turn gas to high. Place 1 cup soaked wood chips in the grill's metal smoking box or in a small shallow foil pan set directly on heat in a corner. Close lid until grill is heated— about 10 minutes. Adjust gas for indirect cooking (no heat down center) and set a drip pan in center. Add another cup of wood chips.

5. Rub turkey with oil. Cut apple crosswise into ½-inch-thick slices and insert into neck cavity; skewer neck skin to back or tuck wing tips under shoulder joints to hold skin in place. If body cavity opening has a band of skin or metal across it, push ends of drumsticks under it. Otherwise, tie drumstick ends securely together with string. Return turkey to wire rack over roasting pan.

6. Pour enough reserved marinade to fill foil drip pan in charcoal or gas grill. Place 3 unheated briquettes over hot coals on each side of drip pan and top with about ¼ cup drained soaked wood chips in charcoal grill. Set cooking grate on grill. Place turkey in pan on grate above drip pan. Cover grill. (Open vents for charcoal. Every 30 minutes, add 2 or 3 more briquettes and some wood chips.) If turkey wings get too dark, cover with foil. Maintain about an inch of reserved marinade at all times in the drip pan.

7. "Smoke-grill" turkey 3 to 3½ hours or until a meat thermometer inserted into thigh registers 180°F. Outdoor weather will affect timing—cold weather means adding more briquettes to maintain grill temperature. Owing to outdoor and grill temperature differences—not to mention differences in turkey size and shape—cooking times may vary. When turkey is done, transfer to serving platter; cover loosely with foil and keep warm. Finish making Gravy. Garnish turkey platter with sage, if desired.

GRAVY:

In a 4-quart saucepan, heat 1 teaspoon vegetable oil over medium heat. Add reserved giblets and neck from Step 2 and cook until well browned, stirring occasionally. Stir 1 small onion, chopped, 1 carrot, sliced, and 1 bay leaf into giblets. Add enough water to cover. Heat to boiling over high heat; reduce heat to low; cover and simmer 1 hour to make broth. When turkey has been transferred to platter, skim off all but 3 tablespoons fat from drippings in roasting pan. Strain broth and discard particles. Measure 4 cups broth. If not enough, add water or chicken broth. Stir ⅓ cup unsifted all-purpose flour into roasting pan with reserved fat, mixing well. Gradually stir in broth and cook over medium-low heat until thickened and bubbly. Stir in ½ teaspoon salt and ¼ teaspoon ground black pepper. Pour gravy into small pitcher; replenish as necessary. Makes 4 cups.

•NUTRITION INFORMATION PER SERVING WITH ⅓ CUP GRAVY—PROTEIN: 34 GRAMS; FAT: 6 GRAMS; CARBOHYDRATE: 6 GRAMS; FIBER: .4 GRAM; SODIUM: 968 MILLIGRAMS; CHOLESTEROL: 86 MILLIGRAMS; CALORIES: 222.

RAISIN FENNEL ROLLS

THESE SOFT, CHEWY LITTLE ROLLS ARE FLAVORED WITH FENNEL SEEDS. THE RAISINS PROVIDE BURSTS OF SWEETNESS.

MAKES 24 ROLLS

1 package active dry yeast
1 cup warm water (110° to 115° F)
1 tablespoon sugar
2¼ to 2½ cups unsifted all-purpose flour
½ cup plus 2 tablespoons semolina
½ cup golden raisins
2 teaspoons fennel seeds
1 teaspoon salt
1 large egg
1 teaspoon water

1. In large bowl, sprinkle yeast over warm water. Stir in sugar and let mixture stand until foamy—about 5 minutes.

2. Meanwhile, on waxed paper, combine 1 cup flour, ½ cup semolina, the raisins, fennel seeds, and salt. Separate egg, placing white and yolk in separate small bowls. Cover and refrigerate yolk for preparing egg wash in Step 7.

3. With wooden spoon, stir 1 cup flour into yeast mixture until smooth. Add semolina mixture and egg white to yeast mixture and stir until soft dough forms.

4. Turn dough out onto floured surface. Knead, adding more of remaining flour, if necessary, until dough is smooth and elastic—about 8 to 10 minutes.

5. Wash, dry, and lightly oil mixing bowl. Place dough in oiled bowl, turning to bring oiled side up. Cover with clean cloth; let rise in warm place, away from drafts, until double in size—about 1 hour.

6. Lightly grease 2 baking sheets. On lightly floured surface, using both hands, roll dough to form a 24-inch log. With serrated knife, slice dough log crosswise into twenty-four 1-inch rounds and place, 2 inches apart, on baking sheets. Cover with clean cloths; let rise until double in size—about 35 to 45 minutes.

7. Heat oven to 350°F. Add the 1 teaspoon water to egg yolk and beat to make egg wash. Brush tops of rolls with egg wash. Sprinkle tops with remaining 2 tablespoons semolina.

8. Bake 12 to 15 minutes or until golden brown. Cool rolls 10 minutes on wire rack and serve, or cool completely and store in airtight container up to 2 days. Warm stored rolls before serving.

9. Rolls can be made ahead and frozen, tightly wrapped, for several weeks. Before serving, thaw rolls 30 minutes; heat oven to 375°F. Sprinkle rolls with a little water, wrap in aluminum foil and heat in oven 5 minutes.

•NUTRITION INFORMATION PER ROLL USING 2¼ CUPS FLOUR—PROTEIN: 2 GRAMS; FAT: .4 GRAM; CARBOHYDRATE: 14 GRAMS; FIBER: .7 GRAM; SODIUM: 92 MILLIGRAMS; CHOLESTEROL: 9 MILLIGRAMS; CALORIES: 65.

Braised Onions, Carrots, and Brussels Sprouts

THIS MEDLEY OF FALL VEGETABLES IS MILD-
LY SEASONED TO COMPLEMENT THE FLA-
VOR OF THE SMOKED TURKEY.

MAKES 8 SERVINGS

2 tablespoons butter

1 (1-pound) package peeled baby carrots

1 (10-ounce) package white pearl onions, trimmed
  and peeled

1 cup water

1 teaspoon fresh or ¼ teaspoon dried thyme leaves

½ teaspoon salt

1 pound Brussels sprouts, trimmed and halved

Fresh thyme sprig (optional)

1. In 5-quart Dutch oven, melt butter over medium heat. Add carrots and onions; sauté vegetables until lightly browned—about 5 minutes.

2. Stir water, thyme, and salt into carrot mixture; cover and heat to boiling. Reduce heat to low and cook 5 minutes.

3. Add Brussels sprouts to mixture in Dutch oven; cover and cook 5 minutes or until vegetables are just tender. Remove cover and cook until liquid has almost disappeared—about 3 minutes.

4. With spoon, remove vegetables from Dutch oven to serving bowl; drizzle any remaining liquid over vegetables. Top with fresh thyme sprig, if desired, and serve immediately.

•NUTRITION INFORMATION PER SERVING—PROTEIN: 2 GRAMS; FAT: 3 GRAMS; CARBOHYDRATE: 8 GRAMS; FIBER: 3 GRAMS; SODIUM: 180 MILLIGRAMS; CHOLESTEROL: 8 MILLIGRAMS; CALORIES: 62.

Corn and Pepper Stuffing

PREPARE STUFFING UP TO A DAY AHEAD,
AND REFRIGERATE. BAKE ABOUT 45 MIN-
UTES BEFORE SERVING.

MAKES 8 SERVINGS

2½ cups yellow cornmeal

1½ cups unsifted all-purpose flour

¼ cup sugar

2 tablespoons baking powder

1 teaspoon salt

2½ cups milk

2 large eggs

½ cup vegetable oil

2 tablespoons butter

1 large onion, chopped

1 large sweet red pepper, seeded and chopped

1 large sweet green pepper, seeded and chopped

1 10-ounce package frozen whole-kernel corn

2 cups water

2 teaspoons dried basil

½ teaspoon cracked black pepper

1. Prepare corn bread: Heat oven to 400°F. Grease 13- by 9-inch baking pan. In large bowl, combine cornmeal, flour, sugar, baking powder, and ½ teaspoon salt. In 4-cup glass measuring cup or small bowl, with wire whisk, combine milk, eggs, and oil. Pour milk mixture over flour mixture; stir just until moistened. Pour into prepared pan.

2. Bake 25 to 30 minutes or until golden brown. Cool corn bread in pan on wire rack 15 minutes or until firm enough to handle. Cut corn bread into 1-inch cubes.

3. In 6-quart saucepot, melt butter over medium-low heat. Add onion and peppers; sauté 5 minutes. Stir in corn, water, basil, remaining ½ teaspoon salt, and the cracked pepper; heat to boiling—about 3 minutes. Remove from heat and stir in corn bread. Lightly grease 3-quart baking pan or casserole; transfer corn bread stuffing to baking pan.

4. If baking immediately, heat oven to 350°F. Bake stuffing 30 minutes or until lightly browned and hot. Serve from pan.

5. To make ahead (by no more than 1 day), follow Steps 1 through 3. Cover unbaked stuffing tightly and refrigerate until 45 minutes before serving; then heat oven and bake stuffing as directed above, increasing baking time to 40 to 45 minutes.

•NUTRITION INFORMATION PER SERVING—PROTEIN: 12 GRAMS; FAT: 21 GRAMS; CARBOHYDRATE: 72 GRAMS; FIBER: 6 GRAMS; SODIUM: 599 MILLIGRAMS; CHOLESTEROL: 71 MILLIGRAMS; CALORIES: 524.

CAESAR SALAD WITH PARMESAN CRISPS

ZESTY BAKED PARMESAN CHEESE CRISPS
TOP THIS CLASSIC SALAD.

MAKES 8 SERVINGS

3 anchovy fillets

2 cloves garlic

1 tablespoon fresh lemon juice

2 tablespoons red-wine vinegar

½ teaspoon sugar

¼ teaspoon salt

¼ teaspoon ground black pepper

6 tablespoons olive oil

¾ cup coarsely grated Parmesan or dry
    Monterey Jack cheese

5 cups salad greens

1. Up to 2 hours before serving, prepare dressing and crisps:

Heat oven to 400°F. In food processor fitted with chopping blade, combine anchovies, garlic, lemon juice, vinegar, sugar, salt, and pepper. In a slow steady stream, add olive oil and pulse until dressing is well combined. Transfer dressing to serving pitcher. Cover and refrigerate until serving.

2. On large baking sheet, place heaping teaspoons cheese, 2 inches apart, to make 24 mounds. Bake 2 to 4 minutes or until cheese has completely melted to form lightly browned Parmesan crisps.

3. With spatula, quickly transfer Parmesan crisps to wire rack, bending crisps over sides of rack to curve into shape. Let cool to room temperature. Place in an airtight container and set aside until serving (no longer than 2 hours).

4. To serve, divide salad greens among serving plates. Place 3 crisps on top of each salad. Serve dressing on the side.

•NUTRITION INFORMATION PER SERVING—PROTEIN: 4 GRAMS; FAT: 13 GRAMS; CARBOHYDRATE: 2 GRAMS; FIBER: .5 GRAM; SODIUM: 214 MILLIGRAMS; CHOLESTEROL: 8 MILLIGRAMS; CALORIES: 136.

TWICE-BAKED POTATOES

YUKON GOLD POTATOES ADDED TO BAK-
ING POTATOES PROVIDE VOLUME AS WELL
AS BUTTERY COLOR AND FLAVOR.

MAKES 8 POTATO HALVES

4 medium-size (2 pounds) baking potatoes

2 large (1 pound) Yukon gold potatoes

½ teaspoon salt

¼ cup plus 1 tablespoon milk

2 teaspoons olive oil

1 sprig flat-leaf parsley
   (optional)

1. Heat oven to 400°F. Place baking and gold potatoes on baking sheet and bake 40 to 50 minutes or until tender. Do not turn off oven. Cool potatoes on wire rack until easy to handle.

2. When potatoes are cool, peel and discard skin from Yukon gold potatoes. Place pulp in large bowl and set aside. Cut baking potatoes lengthwise in half. With spoon, scoop out potato pulp and add to gold potatoes, leaving ¼-inch-thick potato shells. Place potato shells on baking sheet.

3. With electric mixer, beat potato pulp 2 minutes. Add salt and milk and beat until smooth. Place potato mixture into large pastry bag fitted with star tip; pipe into potato shells, spiraling mixture above potato shell line. Brush tops of potatoes with olive oil.

4. Bake 15 to 20 minutes or until potatoes are heated through and spiraled tops are lightly browned.

5. To serve, transfer potatoes to platter; garnish with parsley sprig, if desired.

•NUTRITION INFORMATION PER SERVING—PROTEIN: 4 GRAMS; FAT: 2 GRAMS; CARBOHYDRATE: 36 GRAMS; FIBER: 3 GRAMS; SODIUM: 147 MILLIGRAMS; CHOLESTEROL: 1 MILLIGRAM; CALORIES: 170.

CRANBERRY ORANGE COMPOTE

THIS DESSERT PROVIDES A SWEET YET LOW-CALORIE CONCLUSION TO OUR HEARTY CHRISTMAS DINNER MENU.

MAKES 8 SERVINGS

4 large navel oranges
4 large blood oranges or additional navel oranges
¾ cup orange juice
2 tablespoons sugar
6 whole cloves
½ cup dried cranberries
1 cup red seedless grapes, halved lengthwise

1. Peel navel and blood oranges. Separate fruit into segments; remove and discard white membrane. Place segments in bowl.

2. In 1-quart saucepan, heat orange juice, sugar, and cloves to boiling over medium heat. Reduce heat to low and add dried cranberries. Cover and cook 5 minutes.

3. Stir cranberry mixture into oranges and set aside to cool 15 minutes. Stir in grapes; cover tightly and refrigerate several hours or overnight.

•NUTRITION INFORMATION PER SERVING—PROTEIN: 1 GRAM; FAT: .2 GRAM; CARBOHYDRATE: 30 GRAMS; FIBER: 4 GRAMS; SODIUM: 2 MILLIGRAMS; CHOLESTEROL: 0 MILLIGRAMS; CALORIES: 117.

PEAR APRICOT COBBLER

TO SAVE TIME PREPARE THE SPICED-FRUIT FILLING IN ADVANCE, AND ADD THE SIMPLE BISCUIT TOPPING JUST BEFORE BAKING.

MAKES 8 SERVINGS

FILLING:

9 medium-size (3 pounds) ripe pears, peeled, cored, and cut into ¼-inch slices
½ cup dried apricot halves, each cut in half
⅓ cup granulated sugar
1 teaspoon ground ginger
1 teaspoon ground nutmeg
¼ teaspoon salt
2 tablespoons water
1 tablespoon cornstarch

BISCUIT TOPPING:

1 cup unsifted all-purpose flour
¼ cup yellow cornmeal
2 tablespoons granulated sugar
2 teaspoons baking powder
¼ teaspoon salt
5 tablespoons butter
5 tablespoons milk
2 teaspoons confectioners' sugar

1. Several hours or day before serving, prepare Filling: In 4-quart saucepan, combine pears, apricots, granulated sugar, ginger, nutmeg, and salt. Heat to boiling over medium heat, stirring constantly. Reduce heat to low and cook, stirring occasionally, until pears are soft—about 15 to 20 minutes. Stir water into cornstarch and add to pear mixture. Cook, stirring constantly, 2 to 4 minutes or until thickened. Spoon pear mixture into 1 ½-quart baking dish; set aside to cool slightly. If preparing ahead, cool to room temperature; cover tightly and refrigerate.

2. If filling has been prepared ahead and refrigerated, set out at room temperature 30 minutes before baking. Prepare Biscuit Topping: In medium-size bowl, combine flour, cornmeal, granulated sugar, baking powder, and salt. With pastry blender or 2 knives, cut in butter until mixture resembles coarse crumbs. Sprinkle milk, 1 tablespoon at a time, over flour mixture and mix with fork until soft dough forms. Gather dough into a ball. On lightly floured surface, knead dough 8 to 10 times or until fairly smooth.

3. Heat oven to 375°F. On lightly floured surface, roll dough out to 9-inch round. Place dough round on top of filling, making sure to cover completely. With knife, randomly cut 5 X's into dough.

4. Bake cobbler 30 to 40 minutes or until topping is golden brown and juices bubble along sides. Cool on wire rack 10 minutes. Just before serving, sift confectioners' sugar over edge of cobbler.

•NUTRITION INFORMATION PER SERVING—PROTEIN: 3 GRAMS; FAT: 9 GRAMS; CARBOHYDRATE: 60 GRAMS; FIBER: 6 GRAMS; SODIUM: 283 MILLIGRAMS; CHOLESTEROL: 21 MILLIGRAMS; CALORIES: 314.

CRANBERRY ORANGE
COMPOTE

PEAR APRICOT
COBBLER

RESOURCES

Artisans

Birdhouse Brokerage
(rustic birdhouse, page 100)
P.O. Box 466
Poughkeepsie, NY 12602
(877) 895-1496
birdhouse@frontiernet.net
www.birdhousebrokerage.com

Millwood Toys
(Noah's Ark, page 78)
25025 Hopewell Road
Gambier, OH 43022
(740) 668-2757

Arts and Crafts Supplies

Alabama Art Supply, Inc.
(silver and gold leaf, page 114)
1006 23rd Street South
Birmingham, AL 35205
1-800-749-4741 or (205) 322-4741
Fax: (205) 254-3116

Plaid Enterprises
(Mod Podge, page 114)
1649 International Court
Norcross, GA 30043
1-800-842-4197

Baking Supplies

Bark & Bradley
RR 1, Box 1420
Gilmanton Iron Works, NH 03837
(603) 267-6036
Fax: (603) 264-1138

The Basket Case
(cookie cutters and stamps, page 127)
P.O. Box 3230
Hayden Lake, ID 83835-3230
(208) 664-1261
Fax: (208) 667-1347
www.irresistiblecookiejar.com

Dairygold USA, Inc.
(Irish bacon, page 140)
140 East Commerce Way
Totowa, NJ 07512
1-800-386-7577

Harry and David
P.O. Box 712
Medford, OR 97501
1-800-547-3033

Huntley-Moore Farms
(pistachios, page 130)
5910 North Monroe
Fresno, CA 93722
1-800-700-5779
Fax: (559) 275-5174
Call for free catalog.

New York Cake & Baking Distributor
56 West 22nd Street
New York, NY 10010
1-800-942-2539 or (212) 675-2253
Fax: (212) 675-7099
Send $5.00 for catalog.

Sweet Celebrations, Inc.
P.O. Box 39426
Edina, MN 55439-0426
1-800-328-6722

Williams-Sonoma
P. O. Box 7456
San Francisco, CA 94120
1-800-541-2233

Candles

Illuminations
1995 South McDowell Boulevard, Building A
Petaluma, CA 94954
1-800-CANDLES

Pourette Candle Making Supply
1418 Northwest 53rd Street
Seattle, WA 98107-0756
1-800-888-9425

Primavera, Inc.
312 Michigan Avenue
Decatur, GA 30030
(404) 373-3914
Fax: (404) 373-3914

Decorative Papers and Wrapping Supplies

Cardrageous
345 West Manhattan
Santa Fe, NM 87501
(505) 986-5887
Fax: (505) 988-2358
www.cardrageous.com

Caspari
225 Fifth Avenue
New York, NY 10010
1-800-CASPARI

Dick Blick Company
P.O. Box 1267
Galesburg, IL 31401
(309) 343-6181

The Gifted Line, Michel & Company
(wholesale only)
5933 Slauson Avenue
Culver City, CA 90230
(310) 390-7655

Kate's Paperie
(handmade paper, pages 92 and 116)
561 Broadway
New York, NY 10012
(888) 941-9169
Fax: (212) 941-9560
Send $3.00 for catalog.

Loose Ends
P.O. Box 20310
Keizer, OR 97307
(503) 390-7457
www.4loosends.com
Send $5.00 for catalog.

Essential Oils

The Essential Oil Company
1719 Southeast Umatilla Street
Portland, OR 97202
1-800-729-5912 or (503) 872-8735
Fax: (503) 871-8767
www.essentialoil.com

Lavender Lane, Inc.
7337 Roseville Road, Suite 1
Sacramento, CA 95842
(888) 593-4400
Fax: (916) 339-0842

Fabrics

National Nonwovens
(wool felt, page 112)
180 Pleasant Street
Easthampton, MA 01027
1-800-333-3469
Fax: (413) 527-0456
Call for free catalog.

Floral Supplies

Dorothy Biddle Service
348 Greeley Lake Road
Greeley, PA 18425
(570) 226-3239
Fax: (570) 226-0349
www.dorothybiddle.com
Send $1.00 for catalog.

Eckler's Produce and Greenhouse
(strawberry corn, page 28)
1879 Barron Lake Road
Niles, MI 49120
(616) 683-2509
www.ecklerfarms.com

The Flower Market
(manzanita, page 27)
345 West Manhattan
(Santa Fe, NM 87501
(505) 982-9663
Fax: (505) 988-2358

The Rosemary House
120 South Market Street
Mechanicsburg, PA 17055
(717) 697-5111

Smith and Hawken
(forcing vases and bulbs, page 62)
117 East Strawberry Drive
Mill Valley, CA 94941
(415) 383-4415

Sunfeather Natural Soap Company
1551 Highway 72
Potsdam, NY 13676
(315) 265-3648
Fax: (315) 265-2902
www.sunsoap.com
Send $2.00 for catalog.

Tom Thumb Workshops
14100 Lankford Highway (Route 13)
P.O. Box 357
Mappsville, VA 23407
1-800-526-6502
Fax: (757) 824-4465

Fresh Evergreens

Bald Mountain Farm
P.O. Box 138
Todd, NC 28684
1-800-577-9622 or (888) 611-2129
Call for free catalog.

Omni Farm, Inc.
1369 Calloway Gap Road
West Jefferson, NC 28694
1-800-873-3327
Fax: (336) 982-4163
e-mail: omnifarm@omnifarm.com
www.omnifarm.com
Call for free catalog.

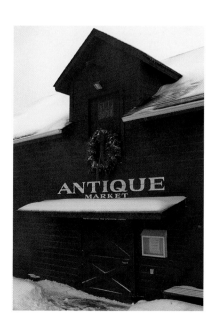

Oregon Roses, Inc.
1170 East Tualatin Valley Highway
Hillsboro, OR 97123
(503) 648-8551

Quilting Supplies

Connecting Threads
P.O. Box 8940
Vancouver, WA 98668-8940
1-800-574-6454
Fax: (360) 260-8877
Call for free catalog.

Keepsake Quilting
P.O. Box 1618
Centre Harbor, NH 03226-1618
1-800-865-9458
Fax: (603) 253-8346

Ribbon

Just Accents Inc., DBA Impressions
225 5th Avenue #419
New York, NY 10010
(888) 389-0550

Midori
708 6th Avenue North
Seattle, WA 98109
1-800-659-3049

Offray Ribbon Company
360 Route 24
Chester, NJ 07930
(908) 879-4700
Fax: (908) 879-8588
www.offray.com

The Ribbon Store
28370 Saint Michaels Road
P.O. Box 967
Easton, MD 21601
1-800-847-8877 or (410) 822-6100

Wreath Supplies

Galveston Flower Wreath Company
(pinecones, page 20)
1124 Twenty-fifth Street
Galveston, TX 77550
1-800-874-8597 or (409) 765-8597

Schrock's International
P.O. Box 538
Bolivar, OH 44612
(330) 874-3700
Fax: (330) 874-3773
Call for free catalog.

PATTERNS

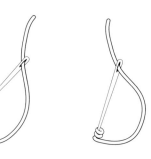

FRENCH-KNOT DIAGRAMS

STAR

CUT ONE
FROM
CARDBOARD.

FELT TREE

CUT ONE FROM GREEN FELT.

ACKNOWLEDGMENTS

COUNTRY LIVING WOULD LIKE TO THANK THE MANY HOMEOWNERS,
DESIGNERS, AND ARCHITECTS WHOSE WORK APPEARS ON THESE PAGES.

Photography

Jim Bathie
pages 4–5, 6–7, 9, 13, 16–21, 23–31,
34–37, 42–46, 48, 49, 52, 54–58, 60, 62,
63, 65, 78, 81 (bottom), 84, 86–89, 92, 94,
95, 98–101, 103–108, 112, 114–119, 135,
136, 142–145, 156–158, 160

Roger Cook
pages 70, 71, end papers

Michael Dunne
page 91

Tom Eckerle
pages 122, 123, 126, 129, 131–134

Peter Margonelli
page 81 (top)

Keith Scott Morton
pages 1, 2–3, 12, 14–15, 22, 32, 33, 40,
41, 47, 50, 51, 53, 61, 68, 69, 72–77, 80,
90, 93, 102, 110, 111, 113, 137

Jerry Simpson Studio
pages 138, 139, 141

Jessie Walker
pages 79, 82, 83, 109

Louis Wallach
pages 146, 147, 149–155

Styling Credits

page 28, antique doors
    Jackalope
    2820 Cerrillos Road
    Santa Fe, NM 87505

page 105, candelabra, wooden bowl, and blue
stool; page 118, glass plates
    Foreign Traders
    202 Galisteo Street
    P.O. Box 1967
    Santa Fe, NM 87504-1967

cover; page 35, Ojibwe birch-bark baskets and
containers
    Lady Slipper Design
    315 Irvine Avenue Northwest
    Bemidji, NM 56601